Direction for Film and Video

Art Direction for Film and Video

SECOND EDITION

Robert L. Olson

SWINDON COLLEGE REGENT CIRCUS	
Cypher	6.3.01
	£25.00

Focal Press

BOSTON • OXFORD • JOHANNESBURG • MELBOURNE • NEW DELHI • SINGAPORE

Focal Press is an imprint of Butterworth–Heinemann.

Copyright © 1999 by Butterworth–Heinemann

 A member of the Reed Elsevier group

 Recognizing the importance of preserving what has been written, Butterworth–Heinemann prints its books on acid-free paper whenever possible.

 Butterworth–Heinemann supports the efforts of American Forests and the Global ReLeaf program in its campaign for the betterment of trees, forests, and our environment.

Library of Congress Cataloging-in-Publication Data

Olson, Robert L., 1925–
    Art direction for film and video / Robert L. Olson. — 2nd ed.
        p.   cm.
    Includes index.
    ISBN 0-240-80338-8 (alk. paper)
    1. Motion pictures—Art direction. 2. Motion pictures—Setting and scenery. 3. Television—Stage-setting and scenery. I. Title.
PN1995.9.A74048   1998
791.43'025—dc21   98-25752
                                                        CIP

British Library Cataloguing-in-Publication Data
A catalogue record for this book is available from the British Library.

The publisher offers special discounts on bulk orders of this book.
For information, please contact:

Manager of Special Sales
Butterworth–Heinemann
225 Wildwood Avenue
Woburn, MA 01801-2041
Tel: 781-904-2500
Fax: 781-904-2620

For information on all Butterworth–Heinemann publications available, contact our World Wide Web home page at: http://www.bh.com

10 9 8 7 6 5 4 3 2 1

Printed in the United States of America

To Gabor Kalman,
a friend indeed

CONTENTS

●

PREFACE

This book details the thinking and basic drawing techniques art directors and production designers need and follows the progress of typical projects from script analysis to setup on stage and location. Even though other helpful books are available that communicate techniques, this book, based on the work experience of a film and video art director, relates technique to everyday work experiences every art director encounters.

WHO CAN BENEFIT FROM THIS BOOK?

Film students can make their projects more professional looking by knowing how to realistically ask for help with location and set projects. Producers, directors, and writers can see how an efficient art director can work with them more effectively. Designers such as graphic artists, advertising art directors, layout artists, and painters and sculptors, can learn how to adapt their skills to film and video projects. Anyone considering a career in video and film art direction can see what the profession is really like.

The second edition includes a lot of new material that will enhance the reader's perception of realistic work experiences and technological advances now available to production designers and art directors.

A new chapter—"Production Designers Use Special Effects"—illustrates how designers utilize digital editing, improved miniatures, and stage and laboratory techniques. Statements from special effects experts and production designers describe concepts and processes they use to accomplish the compelling film effects audiences marvel at today.

Also, chapters detailing the process of design—script analysis, sketching, construction drawing—set decoration, and stage and location work, feature quotes from working designers and craftspeople who share their experiences in solving production problems.

In this book, readers can learn enough basic skills to function as beginning art directors, which are the preamble to using advanced techniques in future careers in the film and video industries.

ABOUT THE AUTHOR

The author has worked as an art director and set designer at the major motion picture and television facilities in Los Angeles, as well as freelancing for many corporate, entertainment, and cable television producers. Along with professional work, the author created and taught a continuing art direction curriculum for the UCLA Extension program, including several one-day design seminars featuring top Hollywood production designers. Other seminars include a week-long course for the Televisa Mexico design staff in Mexico City, a Stanford University Summer Workshop, and courses at The Art Center College of Design, in Pasadena, California.

ACKNOWLEDGMENTS

The author wishes to thank the editors and staff at Focal Press for their valuable assistance in preparing this second edition, and the many talented, creative people in the film and television industry who have contributed their expertise.

INTRODUCTION

This book is for anyone who wants to learn about production design and art direction, whether they are students, producers, directors, writers, or designers from other fields who want to work in film and video. Easy-to-understand practical terms encourage the reader to apply imagination to everyday design problems.

Due to the wide-ranging nature of this book, I have divided the information into three parts: "The Role and Responsibilities of the Production Designer," "Outline of a Job," and "Typical Sets and Opportunities."

Part I illustrates where production designers came from, what a production designer is and does, and basic materials and tools used by designers. Various examples show different projects and solutions.

Part II tracks a dramatic series pilot from script to wrap-up. By following the detailed illustrated instructions, a beginner can learn to analyze the script; research the characters' environments; work effectively with the producer and director; produce sketches and construction drawings; make a model; and supervise the construction, setup, and decoration of the set.

Part III details several typical design challenges met in professional work situations: a series pilot shot on location, a talk show, a new broadcasting environment, and a film commercial. The last chapter tells the beginner how to prepare a portfolio and résumé and how to look for work in the film and broadcasting industries.

THE ROLE AND RESPONSIBILITIES OF THE PRODUCTION DESIGNER

To understand the origin and development of production design, we will first see how the increased popularity and improved technology of motion pictures required better stories and acting, as well as more believable settings. Many designers came from the theater, along with theatrical setting techniques, but as the film industry developed, designers created design and building techniques that satisfied the needs of a new medium.

Part I describes the production designer's responsibilities, basic set elements, the production environment in which the designer works, and illustrates lighting techniques that affect the designer's work.

WHAT IS A PRODUCTION DESIGNER?

Production designers develop a visual plan for an entire production, including sets, props, costumes, color schemes, lighting, and frequently the entire flow of a film. Because film is a visual medium, the "look" the production designer establishes can involve the audiences emotionally as much as story lines and dialogue.

Up until the late 1930s, the title "art director" generally meant the same as "production designer" does today, but when David Selznick gave special recognition to William Cameron Menzies for his comprehensive work on *Gone with the Wind*, this special title later came into general use. Because art directors became "production designers," art directors now carry out the production designers' overall plans for films.

According to Bruce Block, visual consultant for the Meyers/Shyer Company, Burbank, CA:

> Real production design means that you have designed the production. If it's on stage, you design the sets, costumes, and the lighting, and you're through. If it's a movie, you have to figure out what the camera is doing. The visual components are space, line, color, movement, and rhythm. That's what production design is all about.
>
> The production designer has to understand what the movie is about. It's not the plot; it's what I like to call point of view—what you want the audience to feel about the movie.
>
> In *Father of the Bride*, we wanted the house to be a character in the movie. The house was not a backdrop; it was a part of the family like Steve Martin was, so we had to find a production designer who was smart and understood what point of view means and who could bring something to the table besides wallpaper and paint samples.

THE PRODUCTION DESIGNER'S PLACE

The production designer has several bosses: the producer, the unit production manager, and the director. Assisting the production designer are the art director, who executes the production designer's plan; an art department coordinator, who handles the paper work and tracks the budget; one or more set designers, who do the construction drafting; a set decorator; and an illustrator, who creates sketches. The art director and production designer also supervise the work of the construction and paint departments.

DESIGN BEGINNINGS

Production design has a strong history in films. As the popularity of special effects films escalates, the respect awarded production designers, whose imaginations create fantasy worlds inhabited by heretofore unimagined characters, increases as well. In some productions, a production designer can have as much authority as the director has.

WHAT DOES A PRODUCTION DESIGNER DO?

The production designer makes a thorough study of the script, does research, and confers with the producer and director to develop the "look" and flow of color and design from one sequence to the next.

Companies usually retain a production designer for the duration of production. Sometimes producers hire the designer to create a general design scheme and the designer — after providing them with detailed information on the design plan for the film — turns the project over to a staff of art directors and set designers.

Early Production Designers

Who originated the title production designer? In America in 1939, David O. Selznick first bestowed the title on William Cameron Menzies for his contributions to *Gone with the Wind,* which included the direction of some sequences. Before that, art directors were responsible for everything that didn't move, but they didn't have the comprehensive visual authority of today's production designer. To understand how the profession of art direction and production design evolved, let's start with the early development of the film medium.

PICTURES BEGIN TO MOVE

Scholars can argue endlessly about when motion pictures were first invented, in what country, and by whom. We know that in 1888 the Thomas Edison Film Laboratory demonstrated a primitive motion picture device, which was the forerunner of a revolution in popular entertainment.

Few paid much attention to motion pictures at first, because they were regarded as only a fascinating novelty. When movies lengthened, though, the public went for them in a big way. People paid a nickel to watch anything that moved as they peered through the machine eyepieces or marvelled at images on flickering screens in rented halls.

The Audience Increases

The novelty of simple movement wore off before long, however. Motion picture producers saw that they needed to make longer and better films, so they turned to the most obvious source of material – the theater. With the actors and plays came theatrical sets and painted backdrops, as well as theatrical techniques.

Filming took place outdoors to take advantage of free sunlight. Producers perched cameras and sets on rooftops where tall buildings did not block the sunlight. They hoped the wind would not be strong enough to ripple canvas backdrops and flats or flap the dining room tablecloth during dinner party scenes. The audience would laugh in the wrong places. Wind, rain, snow, and ice would slow production and deprive clamoring audiences of amusement and the producer of cash.

Filming moved inside glass-roofed stages, which solved producers' problems with the elements for a while. If they didn't want to hire a set designer, producers hired local carpenters to build realistic rooms. It became apparent, however, that filmmakers needed the talents of set designers. Sets built by house carpenters and decorated by the producer's sister did not look right on film. The camera's eye demanded more.

Movie Makers Move On

Producers ground film through their cameras, processed and edited the footage, and rushed the finished product out to any exhibitor who paid the rental fee. Due to some unpleasantness over camera mechanism patents, producers moved south and west to distance themselves from the patent law enforcers and to enjoy more shooting days per year than the weather allowed in the northeast United States.

Florida, Arizona, and the San Francisco Bay area in Northern California had thriving film studios, but the variety of terrain and reliable weather in Southern California attracted the major part of the growing film industry. An added attraction was the proximity of the Mexican border, which allowed producers to throw their clandestine cameras into cars and to speed across the border to safety, leaving the process servers hired by the camera cartel on the other side of the border.

Versions of Paris

Movie moguls discovered that once they owned a piece of land, they could build their own plaster-and-chicken-wire cities, western towns, and mountains. The lot system also gave movie companies some control over the weather. Many studio backlot sets included cables stretched over the streets that could support opaque canvas covers to provide shelter from unwanted rain and could help simulate night during the day. Overhead perforated pipes could spray rain, which might fall gently or be whipped into hurricane force by motor-driven fans. Some studios constructed dump tanks, into which portions of ships were deluged with tons of water for sea storm sequences.

Walter Winton, a studio staff set decorator during the 1930s, recalls:

> Everything we needed was right there on the lot: upholstery shop, drapery department, electrical, carpenters, painters, greens. We hardly had to go outside unless we needed something very special. The property department was huge; full of furniture and accessories that had been made or bought for other productions.

The Studio Production Line

The studio lots became film factories, cranking out features and shorts on a production-line basis. In the 1930s, MGM had 117 backlot sets, 23 soundstages, and made a feature film a week. Its regular payroll supported over 2,000 employees. Studios recruited designers from the theatrical worlds of New York and Europe. They designed portions of cities on Hollywood lots and in the barnlike stages. If a picture needed a French drawing room, carpenters built the set on a stage and decorators dressed it with appropriate furniture and drapery. The next day the standing set could be dressed as a townhouse or gambling casino.

The lot system delighted movie producers. They wanted to keep production under their close scrutiny. Studios kept dozens of actors under contract and assigned them to emote in one picture after another. Each studio had its backlot versions of the cities of the world. Many of the directors, as well as art directors, were from Europe, so the flavor of backlot architecture varied according to designers' nationalities.

WORK IN THE MOVIES? NEVER!

At first, theatrical set designers looked down their noses at the movies' vulgarity, but many changed their attitudes as the quality of films improved and creative possibilities revealed themselves.

Architects put their skills to work in the film industry, seizing the opportunity to put their imaginations to work on never-never lands of plaster fantasy. They could say goodbye to dull apartment houses and office buildings and live in the magical world of motion pictures.

Studios recruited art directors from architecture schools and put them to work on castles, roads, curving city streets, and villages with town roads and city halls. The management lured designers from the theater and put them to work on musical films.

Both groups had to adjust to working with surfaces rather than internal structure; easier for the illusion-experienced theater people than for the architects who now had to design surfaces and portions of buildings rather than complete structures.

Some Art Directors Became Stars

As the major studios grew, they employed many staff art directors. Supervising or executive art directors guided the art department designers and developed the studio's visual style, much as today's production designers create a look for an individual film.

MGM's Cedric Gibbons became one of the most colorful art department heads. Some say that Mr. Gibbons never picked up a pencil, while others claim to have seen him laboring over an architectural detail. He created the Art Deco-influenced Big White Set look, which became Metro's trademark in the 1930s. Walter Winton remembers:

> Even though we [the set decorators] were pretty independent, Mr. Gibbons kept close watch on what we were doing. He wanted the most rich look we could get; cost be damned—an ideal situation for us. Mr. Gibbons always had the final say, even over producers and directors.

Although many art directors made notable stylistic contributions to Hollywood films, here are several who stood out.

WILFRED BUCKLAND, New York stage designer
  Brought to Hollywood by Cecil B. DeMille in 1915
  Championed the use of artificial lighting.

VAN NEST POLGLASE, RKO's supervising art director
  Studied architecture and interior design
  Designed Art Deco musicals

WILLIAM CAMERON MENZIES, Freelance art director
  Directed some sequences of *Gone with the Wind*
  Awarded first Production Design credit

TELEVISION CHANGES THE FILM BUSINESS

The United States saw its first public exhibition of television pictures in 1927, but not until after World War II did this new electronic medium become as fascinating as motion pictures were in their infancy. Television receiver design progressed from huge revolving disks and forests of wire and tubes behind tiny, blurry screens to an acceptable piece of furniture that dominates many living rooms today.

Seeing this trend, and alarmed at the way people stayed home to watch free television, the motion picture studios developed wide-screen processes, enhanced sound systems, and epic movies to lure people back into theaters. Just to be on the safe side, the studios produced programs for television as well.

Just as theater designers had been reluctant to work in films, many motion picture art directors did not want to work in television. Television had lower budgets, limited production time, and lower prestige.

Make Way for the Sitcoms

Major studios and independent producers jumped on the television bandwagon. Large studios had the facilities and used them to feed television's growing appetite. Staff art directors accustomed to big budgets and plenty of time were now assigned to television series that had neither. They used the big outdoor sets and standing sets on soundstages. Sometimes a series used sets built for feature films not released until after the set had been seen on television. Studios that were accustomed to finishing a picture a month now had to crank out what amounted to a picture a week for television.

Film to Tape Transfer

Videotape recording changed television practices and programming. During the live television days, film cameras aimed at cathode ray tubes recorded broadcasts. These film records – called kinescopes – were the only visual record of broadcasts. Later, magnetic tape recording eliminated that laborious and technically inferior process, and gave the appearance of a live television broadcast when played back. Programmers no longer feared mishaps. They could be edited out much more easily than on a kinescope film. Present day digital editing techniques have improved tape editing as well as film processing.

Improved Technology Affects Art Directors

In its infancy, television equipment made many demands on art directors. They had to work with a limited range of gray values, and had to avoid extreme contrasts of value as well as certain patterns. The old camera tubes could retain an image if held on the same picture too long. The system required high, even light levels, which limited the amount of contrast and atmosphere sets could present.

Motion picture color film process suppliers required the services of color consultants who needed art directors to work within the limits set by laboratory processing. Film art directors had to work with limited color palettes and saw their sets flooded with intense flat light. Mood and atmosphere took a backseat, the same as in early video.

As video and film technology improved, art directors had a greater range of choices. They could use glitter, lights shining into the camera lens, and a more subtle color range. Many art directors chose to specialize as the programming range widened. Some freelancers set up design studios that specialized in situation comedies, game shows, or news broadcasts.

THE VISUAL FUTURE

The onward march of technology, including high-definition video and digital manipulation, will change the role of the art director. Virtual reality systems, which use two small color screens placed in a headset, and sensor-equipped body suits can place viewers in synthetically created environments.

Art directors are already creating new visual worlds, and some predict the day when drawing boards will be artifacts of the past. Perhaps all sets will be made of zeros and ones stored in chips, and some predict the same fate for actors. Will you be ready?

●

The next chapter discusses what qualities art directors and production designers need to have, and how they can put their talents and technical skills to work.

2

WHAT DOES AN ART DIRECTOR
NEED TO KNOW?

Production designers and art directors are supposed to know a little about everything, and have to keep a sharp eye out for detail. Robert Cecchi, art director and set decorator recalls:

> I was working on a period picture which took place on a farm. Some kids had to slide down a haystack and the crew thought you just pile the hay up. Well, the haystack had to withstand six kids sliding down for take after take and the haystack just collapsed each time. I showed them how to pile the hay in layers, like the farmers did to shed the rain and snow.

Larry Miller, Hollywood production designer says:

> When I assemble my staff, I look for people with a high degree of skill. I seem to be *sympatico* with people with theater training where ideas are developed through characters. That's what designing for film is all about. You just can't design a place—you have to design a place for a character and a time.

According to visual consultant Bruce Block:

> A production designer has to understand the characters and the story from an emotional point of view. They have to have great taste and have to understand what happens to things when you photograph them. Some production designers and art directors are more like interior decorators; they don't understand what happens when things go onto film; how film will change a color or flatten things out. They have to know what's going to happen when the cinematographer gets on the set.

AN ART DIRECTOR SHOULD BE
VISUALLY AWARE

The world around us is a feast of images: people, trees, houses, animals, buildings, clouds, and sunsets — all of which enhance our enjoyment of life, as well as provide design ideas. When you walk down the street, look at everything as design. That sign up there! What vibrant colors, and the bank of traffic lights! Imagine it 20 feet high with the lights pulsing to music. Down the street is a building being demolished. The floors are peeled away, revealing a four-story collage wall of decades of wallpaper and paint. It could be hanging in a museum.

Many production designers and art directors carry pocket cameras. One production designer was having difficulty finding the right color and texture for a newly discovered planet to be seen in a science fiction series. She stepped out of her car one day, glanced down into the gutter, and saw a piece of refuse that was exactly right. She snapped a picture of it, had the photo image computer-wrapped around a sphere, and created the new planet, all because her eyes were open to the world around her.

You're in Demand if You Can Draw

Drawing is learning to see. If the art director is visually aware, the ability to draw is helpful, if not essential. Some production designers don't draw well; they have someone else do it. If the designer works at a major studio, the art department supplies sketch artists and visualizers to communicate production designers' ideas in the form of sketches and illustrations.

If you freelance, it's creatively helpful, economical, and quicker to make your own sketches. Also, during the creative process, ideas present themselves that can be worked into your plan immediately. It's fun to see a brilliant idea creep over the top of your drawing board. If you can draw, you can capture it before it gets away.

Another Dimension

An art director needs to understand three-dimensional design. How else can shapes work together from more than one angle? Cameras shoot from many positions. Although a set may look terrific from straight on, how will it look from other angles?

Making sculpture is an excellent way to learn to think in the round. While working with clay, metal, plastic, and other materials, the sculptor rotates a piece, much as the camera roams about a set. The set presents itself from many different angles as the actors and camera move.

What Colors Do You Like?

Bruck Block notes:

> In *Baby Boom* the wall colors were based on Diane Keaton's complexion color and in *Father of the Bride* we keyed the wall colors to Steve Martin's complexion to help make the house a member of the family.

Art directors need to know the physical theory of color and how it works. The human eye's retina has 125 million receptors, called cones, which are sensitive to the light and dark values that the lens focuses on them. The retina also has seven million rods that perceive red, green, and blue. Our brains mix these values into what we know as colors.

This type of color mixing is known as *additive mixing*. Television picture tubes are composed of rows of red, green, and blue dots, which fluoresce in various combinations when struck by the cathode ray beam, producing what we see as thousands of different colors.

Paints, dyes, and inks follow different rules. When white light falls on a yellow card, for example, the yellow pigment absorbs all colors except yellow, which is reflected, making our eyes see the color yellow. This system is called the *subtractive system,* as colors are absorbed.

Color description is a subjective process, so to provide an objective view, art directors provide color chips and color sketches for scenic artists and set painters. Production designers use color for psychological and stylistic effect by keying certain colors to characters, scenes, and sequences. Some designers work out the general color progression from scene to scene before they do other design schemes. If a character's personality is dark, the designer can use low-key colors. If the character is a happy type, the chosen color scheme can be in light values.

DRAFTING: THAT DREADED WORD

Production designers and art directors need ways to communicate building information to cost estimators and construction shops. Construction drawings provide detailed information, as you will see later in this book. Usually, production designers do not do their own drafting but read and understand construction drawings. The set designer, a member of the production designer's staff, does the drafting.

According to Colin Irwin, a production designer:

The set designer turns the production designer and art director's ideas into floor plans and elevation drawings which the construction coordinator can use to get bids on set building costs. Usually, the set designer does not have much creative input, but on a very large project the production designer and art director have to do a lot of running around dealing with producers. I spend 80 percent of my time dealing with producers and politics and 20 percent designing. I usually end up going in on Saturdays on my own time when it's quiet and the phones don't ring. It's the only time I can concentrate without distraction.

Film and television drafting differ from other types because they deal more with surfaces than with internal structure. Architects and engineers are concerned with the mechanics and engineering of buildings and mechanical devices.

MATERIALS

To design a set, an art director needs to know materials and what they can do. What good is a set that cannot be built? Sets are built by carpenters in construction shops and on soundstages, but building plays a major role in location work too. An existing location structure may have appropriate general qualities that need alteration. To save time and money, sets that have no architectural relationship to the location buildings or landscape can be constructed within convenient reach of the location company.

LIGHTING

As part of the set design process, an art director needs to know the basics of lighting. Without light, the set will not be visible to the camera, and because sets should be presented in the best possible way, the art director should produce designs that don't create major problems for the lighting director.

It isn't necessary to know how many ohms resistance are in how many feet of cable or how many lighting instruments one dimmer can handle. It's enough to know a few basic requirements, such as the following:

- An exterior opaque backing should be hung about eight feet away from a window.
- Large areas of shiny surface require extra time (money) and care to light.
- Sets with ceilings can complicate the lighting process.

Make the lighting director your friend. As you will see later, lighting can make your work look better than you hoped, or it can destroy hours of hard work and enthusiasm.

HELPFUL PERSONAL QUALITIES

An art director needs to know how to work effectively with other members of the company. An art director's staff welcomes clear information so that the result will have a cohesive look. Art directors should find the best solution to each problem in a knowledgeable and innovative way. How easy it is to dig out an old set of drawings and have a reverse print made that can be presented as a new solution. Every production has its own needs and requires a different set of solutions.

Be Flexible

Designing a show is like assembling a collage. Directors and producers make changes over which the art director has no control. What if the director asks you to change the most beloved part of your design? First, explain the reasons you designed the set the way you did. Second, be willing to consider the director's view. If you hear valid reasons, be willing to change. After all, the director is the director.

What a Business!

An art director needs to have an effective business sense. Popular belief is that sensitive creative people like us can't balance our checkbooks without help. Some of us can't, but we have to keep track of where the production money goes. Cost estimates and budgets are a vital part of the business. Art directors deal with large amounts of money, at least on paper, and parcel the funds out to many suppliers, all of whom need to be kept happy.

It's OK to Be Disorganized Sometimes

When you're getting your ideas together is the best time for confusion: When you have some facts and ideas for your particular brand of creative process to grind up. Put down every idea with possibilities. When you settle down and the wastebasket is full of terrible ideas, pat yourself on the back for coming up with some brilliant solutions, and, then, calmly set about bringing them to reality. This is the time to be organized.

Passengers! Try to Remain Calm!

Each production is different. When everyone is in a hurry, tempers flare and resentments build. Patient attention to detail is a discipline to practice. Many times things go wrong at the last minute. What if it rains? Is the cyclorama really flameproof? Will the party-scene ice sculpture melt too soon?

WISH YOU'D STAYED ON THE FARM?

Nothing is going according to plan. The 120 gallons of specially mixed paint is the wrong color and the director has decided to shoot the biggest set a week earlier than scheduled. Things work out somehow, and the shoot finally wraps. Don't be surprised if you have to help unstick the elves. After all, art directors are supposed to know a little bit about everything.

•

The next chapter will take you on a tour
of the environment where you will put all the qualities
and skills in this chapter to work.

3

THE PRODUCTION ENVIRONMENT

The television environment presents many challenges to the production designer. Whether the recording medium is film or tape, the designer needs to know how the systems work, how to cope with the limitations, and how to exploit the medium's advantages. However, what the designer envisions and what the viewer at home or in the theater sees may differ dramatically, even though the design team has carefully controlled the set elements placed on the stage or at a chosen location. This chapter describes what basic physical elements designers work with on the stage, how they work, and the picture limitations.

LINES AND DOTS

The amount of fine detail a video camera shows is more limited than the amount a film camera can show. The American video system uses 525 lines of picture information, compared to most of European video, which shows 625 lines; however, motion picture film contains millions of grains of picture information in each frame and can present a very large picture with much detail.

A clumsily attached doorknob plate is about 2 inches wide on the face of a television screen, but can be 8 feet in diameter on a 30-foot-wide motion picture screen. Designers should never allow sloppy craftsmanship to slip by because it's just for television — they should demand the maximum quality that time and budget allow. What if the director decides to use a very tight closeup of a badly fastened doorknob plate?

DIFFERENT PERCEPTIONS

Home receiver adjustment is a major video variable. We have all entered someone's living room when the television set is on. We think: How can they watch such an unrealistic picture in exaggerated colors? Well, they must prefer hot color and low contrast. We have no control over individual taste.

As designers, we must remember that colors usually appear more saturated and brighter to the camera than to our eyes. A guiding rule is to choose paint tones that are a step down in saturation from the color you want perceived on the screen.

HOW DOES THE VIDEO PICTURE GET FROM HERE TO THERE?

The following list describes the way a picture goes through many systems that alter or transform the original source.

- The camera lens focuses light reflected from the set onto the face of a picture tube or digital sensor.
- The picture tube or chips translate the light-dark values and color variations into electronic information sent to camera control equipment.
- The mixer assembles videotape, digital disk, and live camera information into a signal that can be broadcast or recorded.
- The electronic information goes via cable or microwave transmission to a transmitter, where it is transformed into a signal broadcast to a satellite receiver, cable system microwave dish, or home receiver.

BOLD IS BEST

Look at some wallpaper books. When you leaf through the samples, your eyes are just a few inches away from the color and form. Walk across the room and look at the same sample again. Does the color read as a definite color, or does it turn into an indefinable tone? Does the pattern come across or does it become a mushy texture? When choosing colors, textures, and forms, select the definite statements that tell their stories at a glance. Remember how far they have to go.

Now that we have seen some of the system's limitations, and how video pictures get from here to there, let's get acquainted with the environment in which our sets will stand.

THE PRODUCTION STAGE

The production's stage home is a barnlike building containing a lot of empty space. Stages come in many sizes, shapes, and locations, the choice of which depends on the production's needs. If the producer works on a lot with many stages, the production is assigned an available stage. An independent producer shops around for space on lots that offer rental stages. Ideally, the producer consults the art director when reserving stage space. If this does not happen, the art director frequently has to fit the sets into a space that is too small.

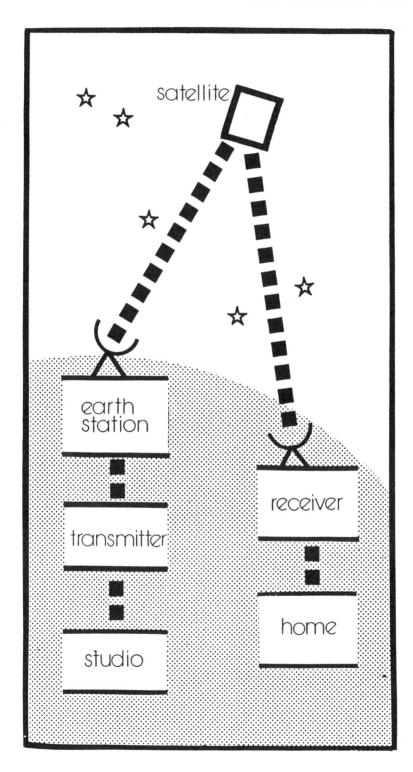

A Sound Idea

Soundstages are quiet, peaceful places when empty. Thick sound-absorbent padding covers the walls and ceiling to keep out unwanted sounds. While filming or taping is in progress, warning bells ring and lights flash outside the stage doors.

Did You Pay the Light Bill?

The lighting designer needs an adequate supply of electricity, places to hang the lights, and a control system. One way to ensure good lighting is to use the traditional motion picture system—suspended platforms above the sets with lighting instruments secured to the hanging platforms. Lights on stands clutter the stage floor, but lighting people frequently use them to supplement the overhead lighting.

Another way, more commonly used for video production in which the cameras need to move freely about the floor, is to hang the lights from a permanently installed grid of pipes suspended from the stage ceiling. The lighting technicians use ladders to take the lights to the grid where they are fastened.

A convenient system is to use pipes suspended by cables from pulleys fastened to the stage ceiling. The lines pass over the pulley wheels to the stage walls, where they are attached to a counterweight system that allows the pipes to be lowered to a few feet off the floor. The lights are fastened to the pipes—a much more convenient system that eliminates ladder climbing. The light-bearing pipes can then be raised to their working height above the set.

The Stage Floor

Stages have different floor surfaces. Some have rough wood which the art director has to cover with plywood or composition material. Stages used primarily for video work have polished vinyl floors that blend smoothly into the cyclorama, a vertical surface made of plaster, wood, or cloth. To create a horizonless effect, the cyclorama – or cyc for short – commonly matches the color of the floor.

Lighting technicians can bathe the floor and cyc with colored light and projections, and scenic artists can paint the floor and cyc with color and patterns. Many large studios have stages devoted to outdoor scenes, complete with dirt, trees, rocks, and shrubbery.

THE ALL-SEEING EYE (ALMOST)

Video cameras convert light energy into electrical energy and film cameras cause chemical changes in film emulsions, but cameras don't see the same angles our eyes do. Our eyes take in a wide angle of vision. Cameras see a much more limited field, even in wide-screen formats.

Aspect ratio is the proportion of the picture – the relationship of height to width. The television picture aspect ratio is 1.33:1, that is, one and thirty-three hundredths units wide to one unit high. Theatrical motion picture film formats take in a wider, more horizontal field of vision, commonly a ratio of 2.35:1. Art directors need to adjust designs to the field taken in by the camera.

Remember Close-ups and Wide Shots

To get a sense of how much of the world a camera eye sees, cut a 3" x 4" horizontal hole in a piece of cardboard. Hold it in front of one eye and observe your surroundings. Notice how your attention is drawn to one small area at a time and how the pictures become a series of compositions. You are not, of course, aware of the whole room or landscape, just a small portion. No matter how lavish your set may be when seen as a whole, don't forget the small areas in your $1 million set, or you may get $1.98 close-ups.

Most camera lenses make what they see appear larger than it does to the eye. Usually, designers make a set more compact for the camera than they would for a home interior to be lived in. If the room were designed to be made life-size, it might look like a civic auditorium to the camera.

The Eye with Blinders

Cameras play tricks on us sometimes as they look at small areas of a set. Watch for the crooked picture, the potted plant that seems to grow out of an actor's head, or the high-backed chair that makes an actor appear to have sprouted wings. While you as art director stand around the set waiting for the coffee break, look at the camera monitor when the director lines up close-ups; this is the perfect time to move that plant.

●

Now that you know where your work is going to be housed and what the camera may see, we'll look at the basic elements of set construction.

4

SCENIC BUILDING BLOCKS

As we saw earlier, pioneering movie producers relied heavily on theatrical tradition, adapting plays and staging techniques to the new film medium. Film and video set designers built on traditional methods as well, adding more sophisticated materials and techniques as they became available.

TYPES OF FLATS AND MATERIALS

Softwall Flats

In the traditional theater, where lightweight, easily transportable scenery is an asset, the basic flat, or wall surface, is a wood framework covered with stretched, painted fabric. This method of construction evolved through centuries of use and is ideal for theatrical purposes. Under a theatrical stage's controlled conditions where the audience is a distance away from the scenery, painting and construction can be bold and lack detail.

Early television production followed traditional construction and painting techniques in the same way that motion pictures did. Early technical equipment allowed little transmitted detail, so stage techniques served the purpose. Contemporary stage, video, and film setting construction, however, uses metal and new synthetic materials as the character of production changes and technical skill improves. The traditional softwall flat lives on in motion picture and video for ceilings and painted backings, where rigidity and durability don't count.

Hardwall Flats

Durable hardwall flats can be used over and over with many surface changes. Carpenters can remove the existing skin and replace it or cover it with new plywood, masonite, composition board, or vacuum-formed plastic sheeting. Hardwalls also provide sturdy surfaces for fastening light fixtures, picture hooks, and shelving.

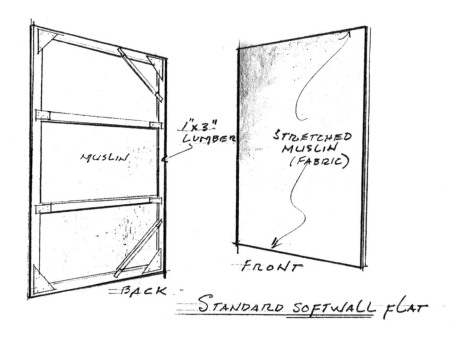

1"x3"
LUMBER

MUSLIN

STRETCHED
MUSLIN
(FABRIC)

BACK

FRONT

STANDARD SOFTWALL FLAT

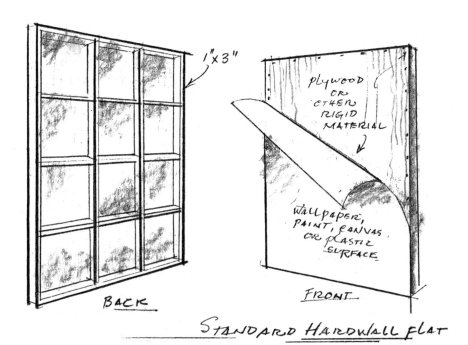

1"x3"

plywood
or
other
rigid
material

wallpaper,
paint, canvas
or plastic
surface

BACK

FRONT

STANDARD HARDWALL FLAT

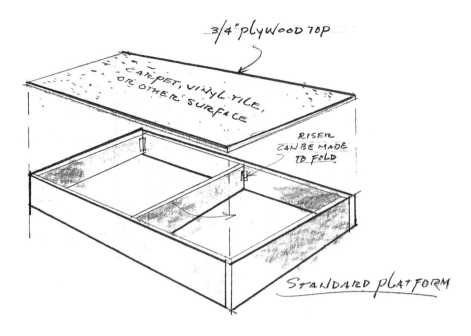

3/4" plywood top

CARPET, VINYL TILE, OR OTHER SURFACE

RISER CAN BE MADE TO FOLD

STANDARD PLATFORM

Basic hardwall flats are made of a framework of 1" x 3" wood set on edge. Lumber sizes are named by the measurements of the rough wood before it is planed down to smooth surfaces. The 1" x 3" dimensions become ¾" x 2½" after the wood is finished. The so-called 1 x 3 is set on edge and made into a grid, each square measuring 24" x 24" on the centers of the lumber thickness. A skin, or covering of plywood or composition board, is nailed and glued to one side of the framework. Standard widths range from 12 inches to 8 feet and heights range from 6 feet to 14 feet.

PLATFORMS

Designers use platforms to create floor level changes. Platforms traditionally are made of wood, but they can be metal framed for extra durability and covered with appropriate materials such as plywood, carpet, and vinyl sheeting.

Plywood sheets form platform tops, which are usually set on folding frames called parallels, hinged at the corners to fold for storage. Standard sizes begin at 4' x 4' and go up to 4' x 10'. Parallel base heights commonly begin at 6" and go up in 6 inch progressions to 4'. Standard sizes, based on 4' x 8' material sheets, provide flexibility and cost-effective advantages. Practical designers combine standard sizes to form raised areas. Nonstandard platform construction escalates set costs, but cannot be avoided in many designs.

Typical Backing

MATERIALLY SPEAKING

Today's designers have a constantly changing palette of materials, compared to earlier times when paint, canvas, and wood were the limit. Vacuum-formed plastic sheets can reproduce nearly any form or texture, and look convincing when applied to flats and expertly painted. Vacuum-form shops publish catalogs of sheets depicting commonly used surfaces such as brick, shingles, and wood planking.

Vinyl materials can give a dazzling look to sets. Many designers design with light to bring out the reflective qualities of new materials, and appreciate the lightweight plastic sheet compared to the former plaster-and-excelsior method of presenting brick and stone.

BACKINGS

Designers use large painted muslin cloth areas to present scenery that does not need to be built. Commonly called backdrops, backings can be huge, covering the walls of entire soundstages, or small enough to cover open doors or windows.

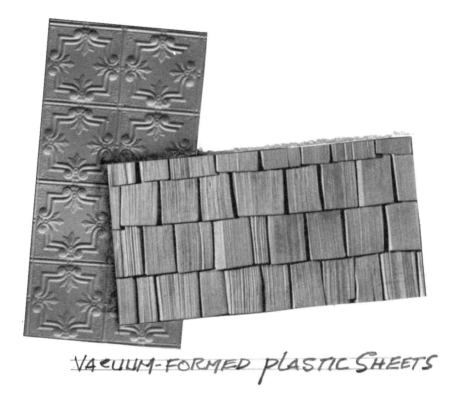

VACUUM-FORMED PLASTIC SHEETS

Scenic artists paint backings from designs presented by the art director or production designer. Backings can be 30 feet high and hundreds of feet long, so scenic studios have paint frames on which they fasten cloth material that can be raised and lowered for the artists standing on scaffolds or the shop floor, if it has a well into which the material can be lowered.

Backings that hang in a straight, horizontal line roll up on wood battens fastened to the top and bottom. Large soundstage backings, which curve around the walls, are usually painted in place by artists working with spray painting equipment.

The Difference Between Day and Night

Some backings depict both day and night and are lit from the back or from the front. In the case of a painted city scene, for example, the daytime appearance is seen by reflected light off opaque painting on the cloth material. For the night effect, the building windows, signs, and a portion of the sky are painted with translucent dyes or paint; when lit from behind, they give a nighttime look.

Some backings are giant strips of photographic positive film. Translucent film stock lends itself to night scenes and is lit from behind, giving a particularly realistic depiction of night lighting. Backing rental houses offer a wide variety of choices.

Moving Backings

Early movie makers had to rely on backings, built like giant roller towels on their sides, to depict moving scenery behind a prop horse, automobile, or train. As techniques improved, they projected motion picture film on a translucent screen to give the illusion of traveling or moving.

●

Not all scenery is made of wood, canvas, and paint. Some settings exist only in digital form, as you will see in the next chapter.

5

PRODUCTION DESIGNERS
USE SPECIAL EFFECTS

With the explosive development of digital technology, many of today's films rely on dazzling effects rather than compelling stories. In this chapter we will see an overview of effects developed from the beginnings of filmmaking, see what technology offers today, and hear from some production designers who use special effects. As visual consultant Bruce Block says, "It's important that special effects be seamless — that they not draw attention to themselves, and that they support the story."

Production designers can choose to use a special effect for several reasons: cost, safety, or fantasy effect. Colin Irwin, production designer on feature films and television series, reminds us about a safety consideration.

> On *Alien Nation* we had a final climactic effect that took place in a steel mill. The director wanted the actors on a giant crane way up in the air. There were lots of holes to fall through—a dangerous situation. To solve the problem, we took still shots of the crane and went onto the soundstage with a blue backing and floor and matted the actors into the still shot with optical and lab work.

For a fantasy film, Irwin designed a new world: "I was working with an illustrator doing mountains and we turned the sketch upside down as a background for a platform we built for the actors, a cost-effective solution for a fantasy situation."

IN-CAMERA EFFECTS

Special effects are not a contemporary phenomenon. Many early filmmakers began experimenting with them. In 1896, Frenchman George Méliés saw that film manipulation could present astonishing results. He made a short film featuring a woman who was there on the screen one minute and gone the next! Méliés first photographed the woman in the room setting, stopped the camera, had the woman leave, and started the camera again on the empty room. When he processed and projected the film, *voila!* – the woman was there and then she wasn't. Of course, he called his film *The Disappearing Woman.*

Frame by Frame

Filmmakers found that they could photograph objects one frame at a time and by moving the subject slightly between each frame, give the appearance of continuous movement. *King Kong*, the 1933 film featuring the famous giant gorilla, used this technique for dramatic effect by single-framing doll-size gorilla and human figures in exterior miniature sets and in front of pictures projected through a translucent background. A later version of the same story used large mechanically operated gorilla figures, and another gorilla film is in production with no physical models at all – the gorilla is computer generated.

Overcranking and Undercranking

To give the effect of speeded-up and slowed-down action, the operator can run the film slower or faster through the camera. Older films, shot at silent speed, have a comic appearance because the film moves faster through sound speed projectors. Special lenses and filters offer another means of altering straight photography.

¼" scale model made of plastic snow and model supplies

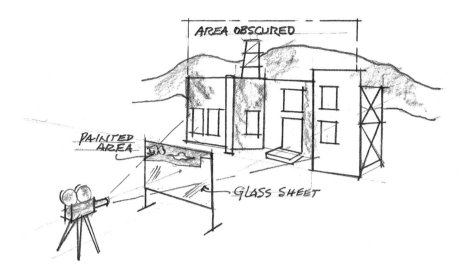

MINIATURES

Miniature settings have important advantages – lower production costs and control over weather and lighting – compared to building a full-size set or shooting on location. Skillfully made and photographed miniature settings are undetectable by most audiences. By carefully calculating perspective and dimensions, effects artists can also create hanging miniatures – portions of the upper parts of sets – which they place in front of the camera.

THROUGH THE LOOKING GLASS

Glass shots, first used in 1907, offer another scene replacement technique. By carefully determining the desired area to be covered, an effects artist paints the added scenic material on a large sheet of glass, which is placed in front of the camera.

MATTE PAINTING

Matte painters paint a portion of a scene, which is photographed and laboratory-processed, to replace a portion of another film scene – similar to a glass shot except that two pieces of film create the effect. Matte painting techniques can save a great deal of production money by eliminating the need to construct large pieces of scenery.

Production consultant Bruce Block compares the traditional matte painting art to the way the technique is used today:

> Every studio had their own matte painting department and just regular movies had a half dozen matte paintings in them just to change the sky or add the top of a building or room. The true craft of matte painting is on the endangered species list. Now matte painting is primarily done on the computer and there are no apprentice painters sitting next to you. The painters coming up now are coming up through computers instead of the fine arts and they don't really understand light or volume or what a shadow is or how to plot multiple-point perspective—hard to plot on a computer. Most of the really good matte painters working today actually paint the scene on glass or masonite and then put it in the computer.

LABORATORY EFFECTS

Optical printers offer a wealth of effects to filmmakers. These devices combine projector and camera so that the operator can transfer different projected images onto one piece of film to produce dissolves, fades, and superimposition of one image over another. The optical printer can replace the glass-shot technique by combining separately photographed portions of scenes.

REAR PROJECTION

In common use during the 1930s and 1940s, backgrounds produced by projected images through translucent screens offered many advantages to the major studio system. A producer could send a second photographic unit anywhere in the world to shoot background footage. Doubles for the actors could appear, as long as they wore similar costumes and were not seen at a recognizable distance. Back at the studio, directors used the background footage behind actors walking, riding horses, in cars, or gazing at the view. Studios kept libraries of background film and used these images over and over again.

Bill Hansard, CEO and Operational Director of Hansard Enterprises, Inc. (Culver City, CA), has seen the advantages of rear projection during production of over 300 feature films, 500 television shows, and 5,000 commercials:

> With rear projection you have the advantage of the actors and crew seeing what is beside them, behind them, or around them. The actors can interact naturally with what is in the background. The crew can do interactive lighting with confidence since they can also see the background. Most importantly, you see in the dailies [next-day film viewing] on the large screen exactly what the scene will look like.

Color Plate 1

Color Plate 2

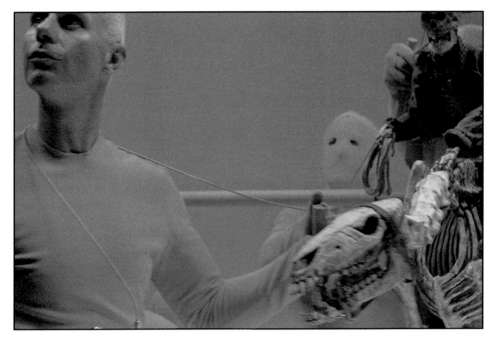

Color Plate 3

Color Plate 4

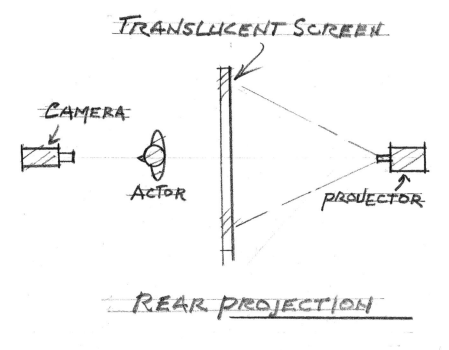

TRANSLUCENT SCREEN

CAMERA

ACTOR

PROJECTOR

REAR PROJECTION

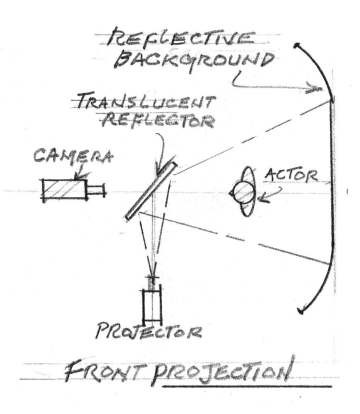

REFLECTIVE BACKGROUND

TRANSLUCENT REFLECTOR

CAMERA

ACTOR

PROJECTOR

FRONT PROJECTION

MODERN EFFECTS

In 1968, Stanley Kubrick's *2001: A Space Odyssey* ushered in a new era of special effects. The film used front projection, computer-controlled camera movement, and extensive use of blue- and green-screen techniques.

Blue and Green Screens

Although rear projection of images through translucent screens enhances many films and saves location shooting costs, the vistas it can present are limited to the size of the projection screen. Blue- and green-screen effects require the actors to move in a void without the aid of surrounding scenery, but this method offers the possibility of larger vistas and sophisticated laboratory processing. The actors' and objects' images are then combined in the laboratory with the background. Bill Hansard describes some of the disadvantages:

> Green and blue screens can sometimes be a false economy. When you are on stage, the blue and green screens go up rather easily, get lit, and you shoot the scene with your full production crew and people or objects in front of the screens. It may have been simple enough to shoot, but it doesn't end there (as with rear projection). What most production companies don't always think about or understand are all of the steps the film has to go through in postproduction. The negative has to be scanned into a digital source, composited with the background, rendered, and finally output back to a new negative. All of this is additional cost and extra time. For every blue- or green-screen shot the process is the same. Additional shots mean more time and more cost in postproduction when the meter is running.

The film *Blues Brothers 2000* has many special effects that used models, green screen, and computer compositing. Available Light Postproduction Effects Supervisor John Van Vliet and staff created the finished effect shown in Color Plate 1. The script required the effect of Valkyrie-like ghost riders galloping through clouds over a live action rock concert stage and audience.

In front of a green background and floor, green-clothed puppeteers manipulated the skeletonized horses and riders (see Color Plate 1).

A separate shot captured the fire-breathing effect produced by flames in front of a black background (see Color Plate 2).

A puppeteer and a puppet horse figure (see Color Plate 3).

Artists and technicians then computer-composited the final effect seen in Color Plate 4.

Front Projection

A specialized projector sends the background image on the same axis as the camera lens onto a highly reflective screen behind the actors or objects. Light levels on the subjects wash out the background image projected on them.

THE DIGITAL PRESENT AND FUTURE

As we have seen, today's production designers have a wealth of techniques at their disposal, compared to the early designers' dependence on paper, pencil, hammer, nails, and paint. Computer technology already produces major portions of feature films and promises to become even more important in the future. If we can produce digital dinosaurs and gorillas today, are digital actors next?

•

In the next chapter we will leave the digital effects world and see basic lighting instruments used by lighting directors and cinematographers to illuminate the production designers' work.

6

LIGHTING EQUIPMENT

A set standing on the stage needs to be carefully lit to make it visible to the cameras and to give it mood and atmosphere. Production designers with basic knowledge of lighting instruments and techniques can work with the video lighting director or film's director of photography to bring out the set's qualities. This chapter describes what instruments produce different qualities of light.

TWO TYPES OF LIGHTING INSTRUMENTS

Stage lighting has two fundamental qualities: diffuse and directional. *Diffuse* light covers broad areas and is flat such as the light given off by a bare frosted lightbulb or daylight on a cloudy day. Focused light is *directional* such as that given off by a flashlight.

Diffuse Lighting Instruments

The following types of instruments give off diffuse light:

- *Scoop* – A large bulb in a scoop-shaped reflector.
- *Broad* – A group of lamps set next to each other on a white surface.
- *Softlight* – A lamp hidden from view, reflecting off a white surface.
- *Striplight* – A row of lamps used to illuminate large areas of backings or walls.

Directional Lighting Instruments

The following types of lights give the lighting director control over the direction, shape, and color of the light beam:

- *Fresnel* [freh-nell] *spotlight* – After struggling with the old thick glass spotlight lenses, which were inefficient and tended to shatter and fall on actors' heads, Augustin-Jean Fresnel invented the Fresnel lens which overcame these difficulties with a series of concentric ridges and immortalized the name Fresnel. His lens produces a beam of light that can be shaped.

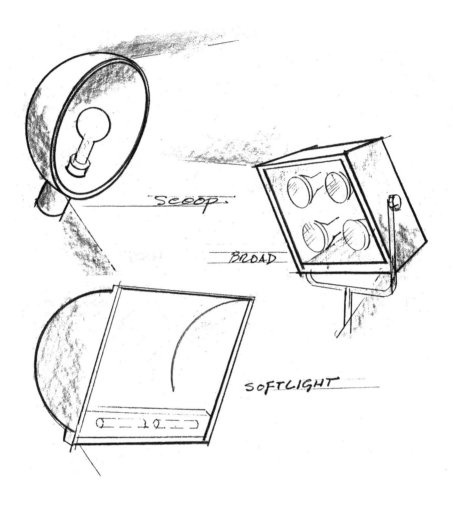

scoop

BROAD

SOFTLIGHT

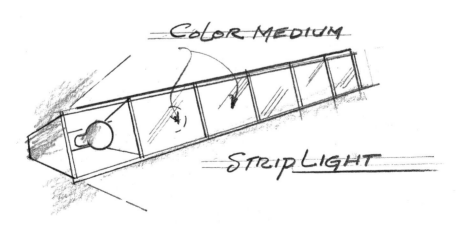

CoLOR MEDIUM

STRIP LIGHT

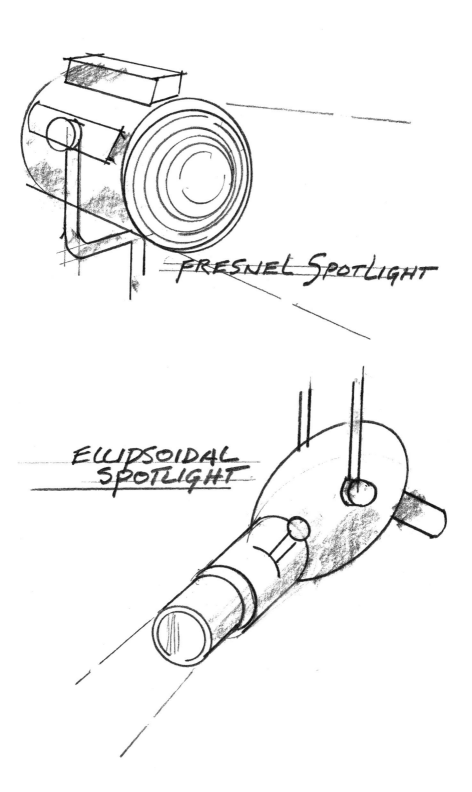

FRESNEL SPOTLIGHT

ELLIPSOIDAL SPOTLIGHT

- *Ellipsoidal spotlight* — This light can produce a sharply defined beam of light. It gets its name from the elliptically shaped reflector inside the housing. Metal slides placed inside the lens housing can cast patterns and shapes on set surfaces.

LIGHT CONTROLS

Long strips of electrical outlets hang in the stage grid. Lighting instruments secured to the counterweighted pipes are plugged into individual outlets. Each circuit connects to a patch panel on the lighting board below where groups of lights can be connected together. Dimmers control the amount of electricity flowing to each lamp or group of lamps, giving the lighting director control of light intensities.

The following sections describe other means of shape and pattern control that help the lighting director, besides the intensity of the light beam.

Barndoors

Each of the Fresnel-lensed spotlights carries a set of four black metal flaps called *barndoors* attached to the front of the lens housing. This set of flaps can rotate and swing in and out to shape the light beam.

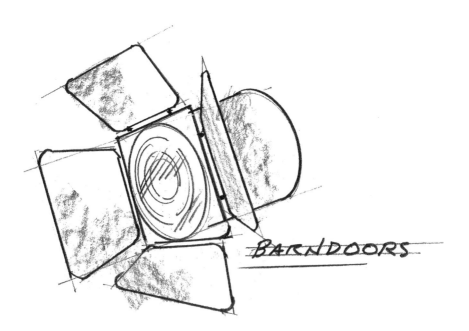

BARNDOORS

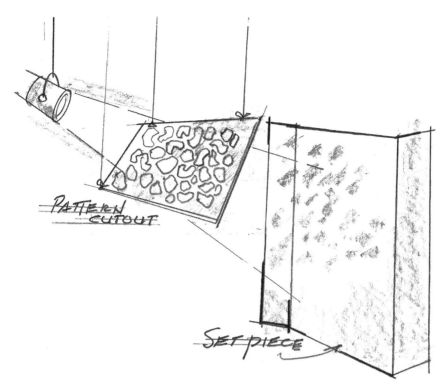

PATTERN CUTOUT

SET PIECE

Color

Channels on the front lamp housing can accept frames holding a sheet of *gel*, short for *gelatin*, which was used before plastic gels were available. Transparent gel sheets come in hundreds of colors, patterns, and frosted mediums.

Pattern

To produce soft patterns on surfaces, lighting technicians hang or stand-clamp a cutout called a *cookie*, or cukie (named after a Mr. Cukaloris), a few feet in front of a light. These wood or metal cutouts carry patterns of window frames, foliage, or abstract designs that can break up an otherwise blank surface.

Flags

To further control the spread of a light beam in front of a light's lens, technicians use flags. These are metal rectangular frames filled with opaque black fabric, which keeps the light beam from spreading.

Reflectors

The unclouded sun produces harsh light and deep shadows. To bounce reflected light into unwanted shadows, directors of photography use reflectors surfaced with

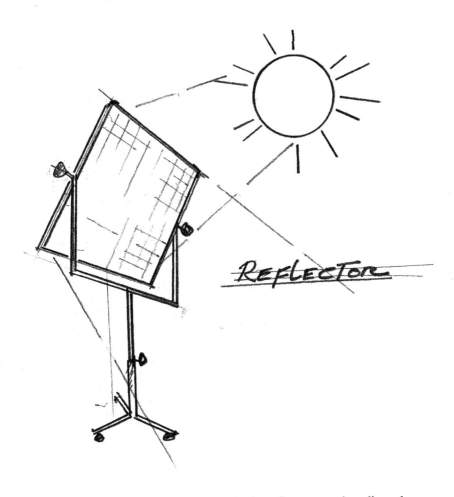

REFLECTOR

foil or white surfaces. Supported on stands, the reflectors can be adjusted at many angles and directions. Large panels of translucent fabric, called *silks*, are stretched over a set to soften harsh sunlight.

●

Now that we have seen lighting's basic tools, in the next chapter two lighting directors demonstrate their methods of lighting a set. See which one you want to light your next production.

7
TECHNIQUES FOR EFFECTIVE LIGHTING

Film directors of photography and video lighting directors work carefully to make settings and actors look good to the camera. To help them achieve the best results, production designers and art directors need to be familiar with some basic lighting methods.

FILM AND VIDEO

Film Lighting

For a film, the director of photography (DP), after discussing the mood, style, and general look of the photography with the director, shoots tests using various lenses, filters, and film stocks. The DP determines the elements and chooses the type of instruments to use and where they are to be hung and focused. Because film photography generally uses one camera and many changes of angle between takes, the DP directs the relighting of the actors between setups as they move from place to place and between wide shots and close-ups.

Video Lighting

The video lighting director confers with the director and video technicians to provide correct working light levels for dramatic effect and electronic requirements. A video director commonly uses three cameras or more and cuts from camera to camera in real time without stopping to relight each time. The lighting director, then, has to light the actors and set to accommodate different angles without relighting.

LIGHTS FOR THE ACTORS

Lighting directors commonly use a triangular lighting configuration for the actors: key light, backlight, and fill light.

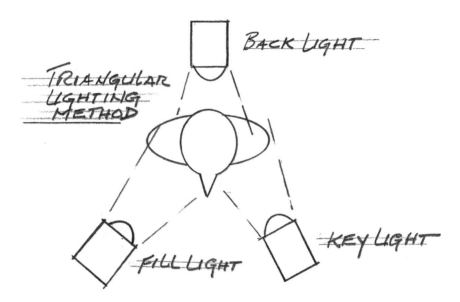

- *Key light* — A spotlight, usually a Fresnel-lensed instrument, lights actors from the front or from a slight angle to provide modeling.
- *Backlight* — Another spotlight directed from the back; this light separates actors from the background.
- *Fill light* — A broad, scoop, or softlight fills in shadows cast by the key light.

Art director Dena Thomson recalls a disappointing experience with bad lighting:

> I designed a set a couple of years ago for a video production set in American Revolutionary times and was most proud of the room where the Continental Congress took place. I did a lot of research and tried to make the set very authentic to the period. A couple of scenes took place at night and the lighting director just totally ignored the fact that the room was supposed to be candlelit! He just poured the light on and that was the end of my set.

DIFFERENT LIGHTING METHODS

Lighting directors Jones and Smith will now demonstrate their ways of using diffuse and directional lighting instruments. Besides having to light the set, they also need to light the actors. Both lighting directors have consulted the director, who has told them where the actors will stand and move, as well as the time of day, which is dusk in this example. Both lighting directors, light meters in hand, stand in the set at the appropriate places, and direct the lighting technicians who hang and focus the lights.

The Jones Method

Jones floods the walls and acting areas of our lovingly designed suburban living room set with the required amount of light per square foot, roams the set with his light meter, calls the set lit, and goes to lunch. This approach get Jones and his crew to lunch early and makes the meters in the camera control system register the correct numbers, but causes much complaining from the director and art director. Jones, however, believes that he has done his job.

The Jones Result

When we look at the Jones-lit set, the ceiling of the room appears to have been ripped off, and brilliant shadowless light floods the interior. The script says that the time of day is dusk, and the heroine is expecting her neighbors to drop over to admire her new sofa. Bright light at this time of day makes no sense at all. Besides, after we carefully designed nooks and crannies into this room and have rummaged through junkyards to find terrific old moldings to go around the doors, the carvings are hardly visible in the video picture, and the set walls are as flat as cardboard. The Jones method has destroyed the character and mood of the set, and does not let the audience sense the time of day.

The Smith Method

Enter lighting director Smith. She lights the acting areas using key lights, back-lights, and fill lights, but the key lights are softened with frost gels, and the backlight comes from the direction of the picture window. Great. Things are looking up. At least the audience can see that light is coming through the window.

Smith directs some low-angle light at the outside of the front door so that when the neighbors come over and step through the door, they are backlit with what we will perceive to be the lowering rays of the setting sun. Aha! It's late in the day. Smith also places a metal slide in a spotlight that casts a window-frame shadow on the opposite wall; another clue that the sun is low. To prepare for scenes that are to take place in full daylight, Smith sets the light levels on the backing outside the window somewhat higher than those inside the set. The smart computer-controlled lighting system remembers the two light levels.

Enter: More Motivated Lighting

We have placed some table lamps at decorative and sensible places in the room. Jones treated them as he did every other object in the set: more things to reflect light to make the meters point to the right numbers. Smith replaces the 50-watt bulbs with which the lamps came from the property rental house with 150-watt bulbs. She then connects the lamps to a dimmer circuit so that if the director decides to have our sofa-hostess draw the drapery in front of the picture window when the sun has set, Smith can bring up the intensity of the lamps to put across the idea that night has fallen. Already the room looks as if someone lives in it.

Firmly Ensconsed

We have placed a pair of wall sconces at either side of a painting. Once again, Jones treated them as more things to make the meters bounce so the sconce bulbs cast their own shadows on the wall, which is impossible in real life. Some lighting directors, the minute their eyes land on the wall sconces, direct a small spotlight on each. The light bulbs then cast their own shadows on the wall, which is also impossible in real life.

Having fallen into this trap early in her career, Smith avoids it by hanging spotlights in the grid above and has the light fall at a sharp angle *behind* the sconces, thereby casting a soft glow on the wall but not on the sconces. We now have candles and bulbs *not* casting their own shadows on the wall.

Smith turns her attention to the set walls. She has the sensitivity and taste to see that we have spent a lot of time finding interesting moldings to go around the doors. She isn't going to let them go to waste as Jones did. Using just enough light, which appears to come from sources such as the table lamps and the front window, Smith brings out the three-dimensional qualities of the room's shapes by casting shadows. However, she does not let the lighting call attention to itself. Smith does not want the lighting or the set to distract the audience's attention from the dramatic action.

Three Cheers for Smith!

When Smith finishes the lighting, the set looks three-dimensional, the audience will know the time of day, the actors will look good, and our carefully selected set decorations will give the audience a sense of who lives in the house. What more could anyone ask? Answer: a raise for lighting director Smith.

LOCATION LIGHTING

The examples here have shown us how lighting directors can make or break a set's mood and atmosphere. The same results can happen on location, where we have less control than on a soundstage. Production designers, however, can have some influence by helping choose the most favorable interiors and exteriors.

Art directors' concern with the mood of lighting on location is the same as for stage work, of course, but flexibility is the key word. Both film and video lighting directors have to light the room from floor-stand mounted lighting instruments because they have no grid in a real room. Also, the light sources have to be cleverly hidden in less space than available on a stage, which calls for much ingenuity from the production designer and art director.

●

Now that we have some familiarity with set and lighting methods, let's meet two important people with whom the art director works: the producer and the director.

--- **Part II** ---

OUTLINE OF A JOB

Now that we have seen the role of the production designer, this part traces the progress of a design project from getting the job to evaluating the results.

We will meet the producer and the director, read the script, analyze the set needs, and learn how to do visual research. Then, based on what we know about the characters and their environments, we will make a sketch of the set and create construction drawings and a model following easy-to-understand illustrations. We will follow the set through construction, setup on the stage, and set decoration, and then we will see where we succeeded and where we can improve.

8

MEET THE PRODUCER
AND THE DIRECTOR

The producer and the director generate the production and the style of a film and are the two most important people with whom the production designer and the art director work. They control the way the production begins and progresses. In this chapter we will see how to collaborate with the producer and the director and some questions to ask them.

THE PRODUCER

First, the producer needs a project to produce and may hire a writer to write a synopsis, option an already-written complete script, or may just have an idea to "pitch" to a studio or company.

Second, the producer needs money with which to produce his epic. He may have his own money, borrow from a bank, or assemble a group of backers who each provide a portion of the production funds. A studio or outside business organization may also fund the film.

Along with other members of the production company, the producer needs a production designer and can find one in several different ways: word of mouth, previous knowledge of a designer's work, contact with the production designers' union, or by chance. If you are just starting out on your career, chances are that a major producer will not call you until you have experience and production credits. Frequently, producers are most interested in your most recent project.

Let us assume that you have worked on a couple of small productions and have worked up a stunning portfolio of real jobs and some speculative samples. After many days of not making any noise at all, the phone rings. A producer wants to talk to you about a project. Those business cards you had printed and passed out to everyone on the set during your last job have paid off.

The producer will describe the project, look at your samples and credits, and evaluate your ability to contribute to the production. Listen carefully, ask pertinent questions, and be prepared at the end of the conversation to be enthusiastic or politely negative. If you decide you want to participate, say so, and get down to business – the production schedule and your compensation. Assuming that you do not yet belong to a union or have an agent, ask how much the producer has in the budget for your services.

You may have difficulty pricing your services. As we have assumed that you have worked a couple of shows, you know how much work you put in and if you felt fairly compensated. Also, because you are eager to get more work experience and want to accumulate more credits, you may want to consider plans which will do just that but will not enhance your bank account.

Plan A: The Points Plan

After describing how exciting a project is going to be, the producer will ask for some sketches. This does not mean that you have the job. The producer may interview several people to compare their ideas. If you get the job, in exchange for your work, you will get *points* – a percentage of the profits after the production costs are paid. If you are willing to gamble, go ahead and participate, but get the agreement in writing. Sometimes your payment may be just more experience, photos of your work, and another line on your list of credits. This may be OK if your samples are still somewhat sparse and you're not worrying about paying your phone bill.

Plan B: The Check Is in the Mail

The producer will claim that the production money is in the bank, and that all you have to do is design the sets, supervise construction, and oversee the setup. A check will be in the mail the day the production wraps. Because you do not know how familiar the producer is with the bank or the U.S. mail, prudently ask for a portion of your fee in advance and the rest on the day the production wraps. At least you will get *some* money in case the production office fails to return your calls later. Once again, decide when experience and samples are worth more to you than payment.

Plan C: The Best Plan

An experienced producer arrives at a budget figure for set construction and art direction services based on the needs of the production. You will be presented with a contract or letter of agreement spelling out what you are expected to do and when. At the time of your signature, the company will give you a check for one-third of your fee, another third at some point during production, and the last third on completion. You will be expected to adhere to the set budget, but sometimes the producer will move money from one department to another, and the art department frequently bears the brunt.

Above- and Below-the-Line Personnel

You will hear about this line — some personnel are above and some are below. Productions prepare two separate budgets: one for the creative people who generate the ideas on which the show is based, and one for the technical personnel and facilities. Individual budgets guide each department and fit into the overall production budget.

THE DIRECTOR

Visual consultant Bruce Block notes:

> If the director doesn't care, isn't interested in the line quality or the color or tonal contrasts, it doesn't matter what anyone comes up with. They might as well be directing a radio play.

Many directors ponder the psychological implications of their work. Art Director and Set Decorator Robert Cecchi recalls one director who had definite ideas:

> When I did *Plymouth*, which was supposed to portray the first town built on the moon, the director sat me down and went through this whole thing about the earth being masculine and the moon was feminine. I didn't quite know what to make of that!

Each director works with the production designer and art director in a different way. If the project is very elaborate, with many sets and locations, the director may want detailed storyboards depicting each camera setup. On a more simple production, the director may prefer to just see an overall view, and work flexibly.

The amount of help directors require varies. Some view the production designer as only the designer of sets and concentrate on the actors' performances and interpretations of their roles. The sets are just the places in which the actors perform.

Film Direction

The film director usually works with one camera and assistant directors who handle the operation of the company on stage or location, which leaves the director time to concentrate on performances. The film director studies the script, breaks it down into elements, creates the shooting schedule, and works with the director of photography and supervising editor.

Video Direction

The video director's job is more technically oriented than the film director's. The control room or truck, where the director usually works, contains many video monitors and other technical equipment. If the production takes place on a stage, the director communicates instructions to the stage manager and camera operators via radio headsets, while calling camera cuts and other instructions to the technical personnel.

Seated beside the director are one or more assistant directors, the technical crew chief, a sound mixer in a booth, and perhaps some production assistants. The producer frequently hovers in the background. Individual monitors display pictures from each camera, graphic material, satellite feeds, and film and tape images.

During a live broadcast, the video director puts the program together on the spot, unlike the film director who shoots pieces of the film and puts them together with the film editor. Video directors can also shoot in this way if the program is not live, of course, and edit later.

THE PRODUCTION DESIGNER
ASKS SOME QUESTIONS

The sooner the production designer confers with the director, the better. In the case of film projects made for television, the director's time is contracted for a limited number of days, so at the beginning of preproduction the production designer needs to ask some questions such as the following:

- *How do you see the style of the show?* A fast pace tells the art director that character-defining objects in the sets will be lost in favor of a general look to establish style.
- *Do you want suggestions?* Many directors don't. They have a limited amount of time and have their own specific ideas. Others do not have a developed graphic sense and welcome composition and camera placement suggestions.
- *What mood do you want to emphasize?* Happy? Sad? The art director can glean ideas from the script, but some directors have their own approach to depicting mood. They may want to go counter to the obvious.
- *Do you have a color tone preference?* Color choice is subjective and it is risky to assume that everyone is going to like your color choices. The

director may want the entire production in gray and blue or in warmer tones, which color filtering can accomplish, but the production designer needs to know.

● *Can you live with the set budget?* Production designer Larry Miller says:

Generally the budget is fairly realistic, but there's never enough money, no matter what level you're working on. I like to be involved in the decisions, although on one film we spent a lot of time and money on a set that was then written out of the movie and never used! The art department coordinator and the computer system lets us know a couple of days in advance if we are about to have a problem.

Because the art director has to sign off on set construction and setup, the director must know what is possible and what isn't so that he or she does not ask for materials and time that are not accounted for. As the old saying goes: "You can have anything you want as long as you're willing to pay for it." Maybe the director will be willing to argue with the accounting department.

●

So now we have met two more variables — the producer and director. They have signed us to design the half-hour video pilot described in the next chapter.

9

HERE'S THE SCRIPT

We are going to work for a producer who is not very affluent and will try to cut corners. The script does not arrive bound in plastic leather with gold-embossed lettering. It has paper covers and is bound with three brass fasteners, the removal of which will allow placement in a loose-leaf binder. The title and author's name are on the first page, as well as the series title, episode number, the producer's name, and the copyright notice.

ANALYZE THE SCRIPT

Freely read the script without making notes. Allow your imagination to see pictures of the characters and their environments as well as the story's general tone. Assuming that you have read the entire first episode script, make notes on the settings.

> INTERIOR – Patty's living room
> INTERIOR – Richard's office
> INTERIOR – Mrs. Harrison's kitchen
> EXTERIOR – The town park
> INTERIOR – Hotel room in Sweden

Small Towns and Flashbacks

We learn that the story locale is Erling, a small town in central Iowa, population 500. The time is the present, except for the scene in Mrs. Harrison's kitchen – a flashback to 1938 – and the scene in the Swedish hotel room, which took place five years ago. To begin sorting out the elements relevant to our part of the production, look at the two main characters.

Patty Johanssen

The writer provides a character sketch of Patty:

> Patty Johanssen, 26, is the mayor of a small town in Iowa. She is a self-reliant young woman, an orphan since she was 14, when her parents were atomized in a grain elevator explosion. Patty lives in the old family home just off Erling's main street. She became the mayor three months ago when she decided that her withering hometown needed revitalizing. Patty ran for office and won the election, much to the chagrin of the town elders.

Now that we have some facts about the central character, ask yourself questions about her environment.

1. What does a small town in Iowa look like?
2. What does an old family home in a small town in Iowa look like?
3. What would have happened to that house in its 75-year existence that could give the audience information about its age?
4. What modernization might be visible?
5. What objects would Patty have collected that could tell the show's audience about her occupation, taste, and general character?

Richard Hansen

The script contains this character sketch of Richard:

> Twenty-nine-year old Richard left the big city of Chicago to pursue the good life (he thought) of a small-town newspaper publisher. He is a new guy in town, unrealistic about the prejudices and traditions of the old-timers who are used to having their own way and maintaining the status quo. Richard lives at the back room of the newspaper office—a small building that houses his office, printing equipment, and living quarters.

Again, here are some questions to ask:

1. What does a small-town newspaper office look like?
2. Would Richard's office be typical, based on what we know about him?
3. What objects would be in his living quarters?

RESEARCH THE CHARACTERS AND SETTINGS

Our producer is not going to give us plane tickets and expense money to spend a week in Iowa, so we have to look elsewhere for visual information. Some art directors keep their own research collections, but have to spend a lot of time and money collecting, maintaining, and housing the material.

It is, however, impossible for most individuals to collect enough material to cover all their needs. Art directors generally have some books and photographs collected from previous projects that may come in handy again. Basic books, such as atlases, architectural standards, lettering, pictorial encyclopedias, and volumes that are of particular interest to the individual, serve the designer well.

Use Your Library Card

Most sizable public libraries maintain reference section picture files that contain photographs and drawings. Remember that an illustrator's view of small towns in Iowa can be misleading, compared to a documentary photograph. Paintings and drawings can give valuable hints on color and composition, but do not necessarily represent the reality that should be your design's starting point. Also, the cataloging systems used in libraries may unintentionally hide the pictures you are looking for because they are set up for *word* rather than *picture* use.

Specialized Libraries

In the early days of motion picture production this same problem cropped up, so studios assembled their own specialized visual material libraries. These collections contained research material for script writers, but also held picture material for set designers and art directors. A few major studios have retained these libraries, and others have sold their research collections to individuals who continue to provide research services for an hourly fee.

Look Out for the Toaster Experts

When looking for and using research material, be assured that someone in the viewing audience will notice an error in time placement; for sure, someone will notice the 1955 toaster in your 1949 kitchen. Use objects and decorating styles that were present *before*, or contemporary *with* the period in which your sets are supposed to exist, but never *after* the period, because these objects and styles would not have existed then.

Mail Order Catalogs

As indicators of objects and styles in current use during a specific period, popular mail order catalogs are very reliable. They accurately document mass taste and provide guides to common objects such as stoves, furniture, and bric-a-brac. Family photo albums provide exact recordings of everyday life as well.

Don't Take Anyone's Word for It

There's no substitute for original sources, firsthand observation, and the camera. Don't guess what something looks like. Spend time searching out reality. Then, put your own interpretation on it.

●

Now that we have found out how to gather general information for further scrutiny, in the next chapter we will see how to use these materials.

10

USING RESEARCH MATERIALS

This is how Colin Irwin, a production designer, starts his projects:

> First I read the script to get a feeling for the story and try to find something that summarizes what the script says to me. Then I pull out research material. I keep a cutting file from *Architectural Digest, Metropolitan Home,* and whatever magazines that have inspirational material. For specific information, I go to reference libraries.

Now that you have a pile of research material staring you in the face, the time has come to sort it. There it is—books, photographs, clippings, fabric samples, color chips, family albums, and some catalogs. First, organize the pile so that you can find what you need for each set.

Here are some general categories:

Iowa, general landscape
Small towns (general)
Houses, exterior (Patty)
Houses, interior (Patty)
Newspaper offices (Richard)
Kitchens, 1939 (Mrs. Harrison)
Parks, Iowa small town
Hotel rooms (Sweden)

Go through the pile and place the material in subject-labeled folders. Then, while you're making sketches, you can find individual categories without having to sift through the entire stack. Clear some flat workspace in your vast studio or on the breakfast bar where you can lay out the folders.

DESIGNING FROM MATERIALS

Iowa, General Landscape

For this project, the general landscape material will be of limited use because most of the sets are interiors. The things in this folder will be useful when it's time to find or create backings to use outside doors and windows. If this were a film feature, this file would be one of the most useful because a film production on location would be concerned with the appearance of the landscape more than a studio production with just interior sets.

The most we will need to see of the landscape – other than generic scenes used as stock program opening establishing shots – are some glimpses through doors and windows and in the park scenes to be shot on the stage. If individual houses seen in exterior photography are identified as places where specific characters live, you will need to take detailed photographs of these structures from many angles in case you will need to reproduce portions of them on stage.

Small Towns, General

The material in this folder is similar in nature to the general landscape group, but it shows buildings and architectural style and detail, again useful for background design and painting.

Most old towns undergo "modernization" along the way. If you were to design these lower facades to look like their original condition, what would you do to alter them?

**Is this a contemporary house design, or an updated old house? What do you
see in this photograph that makes you think so?**

Houses, Exterior (Patty)

Look at the forms of the houses, and the materials, colors, and textures created by
occupants and weather conditions. Is the house covered with aluminum siding,
which is wider than the original wood siding? Has the house been painted many
times, revealed by peeling coats of paint? Is the house in keeping with Patty's
background as you know it from the script? What kinds of downspouts, roof
surfaces, and chimneys do you see? Is the house well-kept? What kind of shrubbery
grows around the house?

Houses, Interior (Patty)

Our study of the script tells us that only the front hall, the inside of the front door,
and the living room will be needed for the pilot episode. This does not mean that
you cannot use elements from other rooms if they seem appropriate and useful for
the two areas you need to create. Patty's living room might be a combination of old
and new, because this is the house in which she has lived all her life. Therefore, the
room would probably contain old and new furniture and objects.

Look at the walls and windows in your research photographs. Houses change
and have their own personalities. Do you see a combination of tall older windows
and aluminum-framed picture windows? Are the walls papered? What are the

colors and patterns? Has someone installed printed wood panels over the original wall surfaces? What kinds of moldings show at the baseboards and door frames? Are the floors carpeted wall-to-wall or does wood flooring show around the edges of area rugs?

Study the ceilings because you may want to include portions to keep the cameras from overshooting the upper parts of the set. Observe the styles of furniture in your photographs. Perhaps Patty's old sofa would have been reupholstered in a contemporary fabric.

Newspaper Offices (Richard)

When Richard took over the newspaper building, how would he have changed it? Would he have left the inside and outside as he found it? Once again, imagine his character, age, and future hopes as described by the scriptwriter. How would he alter the office and living quarters?

Because the previous owner retired at the age of 75, he probably was still using the same typesetting equipment and press he had started out with. Richard might put in more contemporary devices. His living quarters would reflect his all-absorbing interest in the business but not so much in his quarters.

Mrs. Harrison's Kitchen (1938)

Back into the past with this set. You have found reliable research material and have studied it thoroughly, watching out for the old demon — the new toaster in the old set.

Pay attention to the windows in the research photographs. Curtains and frames help establish a sense of time. You will need a backing outside the windows, so think about using a wood fence in front of a stock generalized small town scene. Perhaps a miniature water tower between the fence and the backing would help give depth to the exterior view.

Refer to the script to see if the characters enter and exit through interior doors. If they do, provide suitable *wild* (movable) walls that the camera can see through open doors.

Parks, Small Town

Instead of walls, floor, and ceilings, these photographs show ground, sky, and vegetation. To be convincing, exteriors on stages call for much thought and skill. If you try to get by with some plastic tree trunks and wrinkled grassmats, expect to hear cries of rage from the director. Select research material that shows examples of local vegetation. Remember that avocado trees do not grow in Iowa parks.

Don't try to create a forest. Create the illusion of a larger park using economical means such as foreground shrubbery and overhead branches. The audience will believe that the rest of the trees and shrubs are just outside the picture. If the plantings do not have to be in place for more than a day or two, cared-for live plants will work. Realistic artificial plants are more practical, and chemically preserved natural foliage is available at larger production centers.

Look at the ground surfaces in your photographs. A park can have large areas of gravel or concrete, which is a way to avoid the wrinkled grassmat disaster. Some stages at large studios have real dirt floors, but because you may not have that advantage, think of ways to cover a vinyl-covered stage floor so that it "reads" as grass, dirt, or concrete.

What do you see beyond the ground surface? A possibility is a view of the town in the distance, depicted on a painted backing. Another could be a building beside the park coming into the camera frame at an angle.

If you decide to use a backing, think carefully about how to blend the ground surfaces into the painted scene so that the camera does not see an obvious line where the ground meets the sky. A built-up hill can solve that problem, or irregular rows of shrubbery, which diminish in size as they move away from the camera. Be sure that the lighting director does not allow the shrubbery to cast shadows onto the painted backing.

Place some three-dimensional objects in the set to give the director and actors opportunities for action. A set of swings, some benches, a water fountain, and picnic tables will provide visual interest as well.

Hotel Rooms, Sweden

Proceed the same way, from general to specific, with this set. The hotel might be an old building. Find furniture that says *Sweden*. A tile corner stove would say a lot about the locale. What do old Swedish hotel windows look like? How are they different from American hotel windows?

If you can't find a backing that depicts a Swedish city, perhaps you can squeeze the set budget to permit having one painted from your research photographs. If this lavish approach is not possible, put a piece of tiled roof outside the window with the sky showing behind it. Would it be too much to put an appropriately sized Swedish flag waving in a concealed electric-fan breeze above the roof? If the little water tower worked outside Mrs. Harrison's kitchen window, a flag might do the job in Sweden.

NONSPECIFIC RESEARCH

All research material does not have to be of specific objects or places. Production designer Larry Miller uses general material for inspiration:

> Sometimes I find a picture that has just the right color sense for the film, but has nothing to do with the story. When I can't decide on a color for something, I can go to the picture and find the answer.

●

Now that you have some visual ideas rattling around in your head, put them together and make them visible to others. Turn to the next chapter to see how.

11

MAKE SOME SKETCHES

A good way to put collected images together and communicate visual ideas is to make sketches. Later, we will make a simple model and construction drawings based on these sketches, but for now, just freely put your ideas on paper — successes and failures — and the set sketch to show your client will come together. This chapter shows you how to make a perfectly acceptable perspective sketch.

Remember that sketches are not meant to hang in a museum (unless you become famous). Regard them as steps in the design process, as production designer Larry Miller illlustrates: "On the film *Flamingo Kid*, I did presentation boards with a color scheme for the Eldorado Club set — yellow and gold. The producer said, 'I'm not too crazy about gold!' so I did something else."

MATERIALS

Tracing Paper

No matter what your fifth-grade art teacher told you, it's OK to trace. Don't draw on opaque paper. You'll have to transfer everything to tracing paper anyway, because it's more expensive and difficult to duplicate sketches done on opaque paper. Tracing paper's major quality is its transparency. If you spend a lot of time on a sketch, and want to keep only part of it, just trace the best parts onto another piece and throw the bad parts away. Also, opaque paper doesn't work in a blueprint machine.

Don't Judge Tracing Paper by Its Cover

Tracing paper comes in rolls, sheets, and pads. The price of a roll seems high, but it's the cheapest in the long run because you do not pay for cutting, padding, and covers. You can tear the right size piece of paper off the roll by placing it under a metal edge, or against the side of the kitchen table, or by cutting it with scissors.

Save the Best for Later

It's not necessary to buy fine-quality paper for sketching, no matter what the salesperson may say. Save the tough better-quality paper for final construction drawings because it will have to stand up to a lot of erasing and will travel through the chemical mists and rollers of a blueprint machine.

Drafting Tape

Buy a roll of drafting tape, which is similar to masking tape. This useful stuff will come in handy later when you convert your sketch into construction drawings, and when you need to tape a good idea to the wall. Never use pushpins to fasten drawings to your drawing board. Pins make holes that can ruin beautiful lines and break lead points.

A Little Talk About Pencils

Unless you feel insecure without a large jar bristling with pencils, all you really need for sketching is a soft lead pencil such as 4B or 5B. Soft lead works best because it provides little resistance to being zipped across paper, makes clearly reproduceable lines, and can be smudged and smeared for professional-looking shading. All you need for that is your thumb.

PATTY'S LIVING ROOM

After collecting and studying your research materials, you have an impression of Patty's living room. Remember that a set is not a real room; it is just a collection of information based on what you know about the time period, the town, and how you visualize Patty's character. Tell the audience that only Patty could live in this set — not her uncle or grandmother.

Give the room three-dimensional character for the camera so that it does not look like a painted theatrical backdrop. Set the windows and doorways in alcoves, use picture rails to give the walls character, and show logical changes in floor level. Don't jam all the furniture against the walls, but group tables, chairs, and sofas out in the room, which will give the director and actors opportunities for action. Remember that all the furniture does not have to face the camera. Foreground pieces for the camera to look past enhance the real-room feeling.

The audience must sense that the rest of the house is there, but they just don't see it. Provide open doors, which give the camera glimpses of other rooms that may exist only as a flat with a picture hanging on it.

How Big?

Cameras make sets look larger than they appear to the eye, so if you want a wall to look 10 feet wide, you might make the wall 9 feet wide. If unsure about room sizes, measure some familiar rooms for reference. When making sketches of sets, don't worry too much about exact dimensions, but make your drawing represent the set in general size and feeling. When you have designed some sets and see them sitting grandly on stage, you will develop a sense of how sketch appearances compare to the result.

Remember that the producer and director, as well as other members of the company, will look at your preliminary sketches to get an impression of size, mood, and playing areas. When the producer tells you to make construction drawings, keep in mind what they have seen in the sketches so that you will not hear the dreaded words: "I didn't know it was going to look like that!"

Perspective

To make the sketch look three-dimensional, you need to use a simple system of drawing called *one-point perspective*. Don't be alarmed at that dreaded word; it's just a mechanical device that will serve you well all the days of your design life. Tape the corners of an 18" x 24" piece of tracing paper to your drawing surface. If your

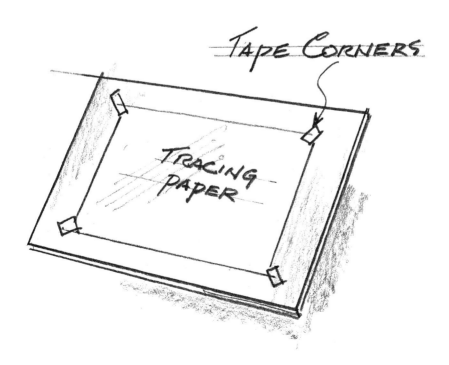

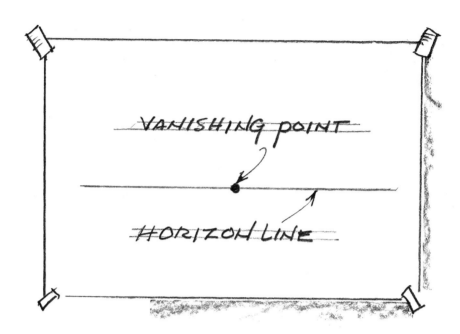

sketch is smaller than 18" x 24", clients at production meetings will not be able to see it clearly from across the room. A reducing copying machine can make smaller versions of the sketch, which you can distribute at the meeting.

Slightly below the center of your taped-down tracing paper, draw a horizon line across the paper. At the center of the paper, make a dot. This dot represents the vanishing point where all extended lines representing the tops and bottoms of the right- and left-side set walls will vanish. In this simple perspective system, the lines representing the top and bottom of the set's back wall will be above and below and parallel to the horizon line.

Visualize how much space the finished drawing will occupy. Before you begin drawing the set walls, remember that your finished drawing should be roughly centered on the paper with about two inches of border around the edges. If you start drawing down in one corner, you will end up with vast areas of blank territory on the rest of the paper.

Draw the Back Wall

About six inches above the horizon line with the dot, draw a line to represent the top of the back (upstage) wall, and draw another line about four inches below the horizon line to represent the bottom of the upstage wall. Then draw vertical lines defining the length of the upstage wall. Now draw longer vertical lines a few inches to the right and left of the lines indicating the ends of the upstage wall and connect the tops and bottoms to the top and bottom corners of the upstage wall. Place these

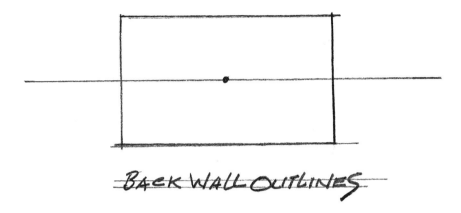

angled lines by putting your ruler or straightedge on the dot, line the straightedge up on the appropriate corner of the upstage wall and end the line at the tops and bottoms of the vertical lines. Voila! You have now created what looks like a three-sided box with no top, bottom, or front.

Add a little stylized human figure near the front, which will give a size comparison for the room. From now on, be sure that all parallel lines moving away from the front end at the vanishing point dot if extended.

What Do We Do with the Box?

Perspective wasn't so hard, now, was it? Surely you can see that the foundation of Patty's living room has emerged. Draw doors and windows and remember that the ps and bottoms of lines indicating these additions vanish at the horizon line the same way the tops and bottoms of the side walls do. Establish other dots on the horizon line for the vanishing points of objects you draw at angles.

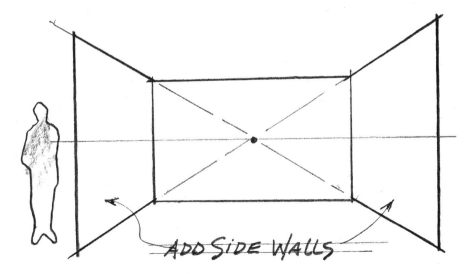

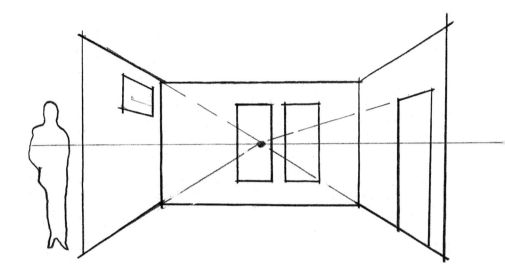

Don't draw a complete ceiling, because this surface can complicate the lighting designer's job, but you might put in a piece of ceiling at the back to keep the camera from overshooting the set and to give the idea that the rest of the ceiling exists. Add furniture, pictures, and other set dressing, but keep the perspective rule in mind .

Give your drawing some freehand character, thumb-smudge some of the lines and use the side of your pencil lead to create shadows. Take a hard look at the drawing to see if you need to make some tentative lines bolder. Some careless abandon at this point will remove the tight wiry look that mechanically produced sketches can have. It will also make the company certain that they have hired a talented designer who knows how to make lively sketches.

GET COST ESTIMATES

You, the designer, need to know if your set fits the production budget. Later, when you have finished the construction drawings, you will take them to construction shops to get firm bids. For now, however, take your uncolored tracing paper sketch to some shops and ask them to give you preliminary cost information. Most shops are glad to do this, because you may ask them for a construction bid later.

The construction shop bases their quick estimate on dollars per running foot of wall and how much detailing they see. Their bid will not include any set dressing, so you will need to visit property rental shops to get estimates. If you find that the estimates average higher than your budget, eliminate some set elements such as

fancy door moldings, platforms, or jogs in walls. The construction shop supervisor can illustrate other ways to bring costs down, such as using already-built stock flats. Make the producer aware of changes you need to make.

No Coloring Yet

Stifle the urge to color your original sketch at this point. Take the sketch to a blueprint shop and get prints on paper. They are not expensive, so get some extras in case of coffee spills. You will be thrilled to see how much the printing process enhances your sketch. Shops offer blue-, black-, and brown-line prints. Trim and mount the print on mat board with spray glue, rubber cement, or dry-mount tissue.

What Colors?

Have a color plan in mind. Decide what general color impression the set should have. Unless the set walls need to be very colorful to suit the characters and story, use grayed-down tones to keep the set from calling attention to itself and to provide a telling but unobtrusive background. Save bright colors for appropriate accents in the furniture and other set decoration.

Use markers, crayons, or pencils to color your mounted sketch. Liquid mediums can make the print wrinkle. If you need to make color copies of the finished sketch, laser copying machines do an excellent, faithful job.

THE TOUR BUS IS LEAVING

Sketch presentation can cause butterflies in the stomach, but if you have done your homework, carefully analyzed the problems, and accurately estimated costs, relax and see what happens. Give a guided tour around the drawing, fabric swatches, and color samples. Point out camera-angle opportunites. Chances are that your worst fears will not be realized and you will not have to slink out of the room with your sketches under your arm. Be willing to listen to suggestions and profit by them. It's possible you may have overlooked something.

●

When your sketch has impressed one and all, it's time to convert your design into construction drawings that will tell the carpenters what to build. To make the construction drawings, you will need a few more tools, which are described in the next chapter.

12

TOOLS FOR CONSTRUCTION DRAWINGS

The producer and director think your sketches are inspired and have told you to go ahead with the pilot project. What now? Do you just take the sketches to the construction shop and tell them to build it? No. Building from sketches is an emergency measure when time is short and experienced set builders can tackle the job.

We are not going to work that way—taking what seems to be the easy way out. We are going to do it the right way by making construction drawings for bids. For this stage, you will need some more aids—more pencils, a T-square, an architect's scale, and triangles.

YOUR DRAWING BOARD

A drawing board should be flat, have perfectly straight edges, and possess corners that form 90° angles. Get the largest size board you can accommodate. Boards smaller than 24" x 30" are not useful for making construction drawings. Boards 30" x 40" or larger serve most purposes. A table and a couple of blocks to prop up your board work, but if you want to spend more money, get a board with legs or a pedestal. Make sure the board doesn't shake when leaned on.

Be kind to that piece of wood. Remember that dents or holes will make dents and holes in your drawings when your pencil passes over the tracing paper. Art supply stores sell many types of cover materials to protect the wood's surface. Once again, don't use pushpins to fasten your drawings. Later, as projects roll in, you may want to invest in a drafting table with an adjustable, slanted surface.

DRAFTING PAPER

Remember, we said earlier that tracing paper by the roll is the best way to go. Buy good quality paper for finished construction drawings, but you can use less-expen-

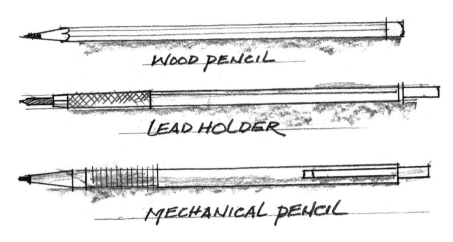

WOOD PENCIL

LEAD HOLDER

MECHANICAL PENCIL

sive paper for preliminary drawings unless you expect to do a lot of erasing. Art supply stores sell tracing sheets with printed borders and title blocks. These sheets cost more and look impressive, but force you to work within the border confines, unlike roll tracing paper which lets you draw your own borders and title blocks.

Another type of tracing paper has a ⅛" or ¼" grid printed in light blue that does not reproduce in the blueprint process; the grid is useful as a guide when your T-square, architect scale, and triangles are not available.

PENCILS

If you use ink, fiber-tipped, or ballpoint pens to make construction drawings, erasing is impossible. The following are three common types of pencils and lead holders.

1. *Wood-bodied lead pencils* are the cheapest, but require constant sharpening and replacement. A pencil extender can squeeze the last bit of use out of a short pencil. Hand-crank and electric sharpeners, knives, and sandpaper blocks work on this pencil.
2. *Metal lead-holders* use the same lead thicknesses as the wood type, but need only replacement of the lead in the holder. Sharpen these leads with a sandpaper block, knife, or drafting lead pointer.
3. *Mechanical pencils* commonly use 0.5 or 0.7 millimeter leads which remain the same width and renew themselves by a push on the top of the pencil; no sharpener needed. Each lead thickness requires its own holder.

Choose whichever type of pencil seems right for you. Start with two lead hardnesses: 2H for heavy lines, and 4H for the light lines. Everyone has favorites.

Retired art directors rocking on the porch at The Home for Old Art Directors while away many hours arguing the pros and cons of the lead pencil, lead holder, and mechanical pencil. Some like to use only one lead hardness, and, by bearing down with various pressures, make different line weights. Others argue for many pencils holding several lead types.

ERASERS

Erasers such as the Pink Pearl™ work fine for eliminating sketch and construction-drawing pencil lines. If you plan to do a lot of erasing and hate to throw a drawing in the wastebasket, invest in an electric eraser. This device will make everyone think you are an experienced pro or wonder if you make a lot of mistakes.

YOUR T-SQUARE

T-squares are guides for drawing smooth horizontal lines and serve as plastic triangle bases for vertical lines or lines at angles. For construction drawing, a plain wood T-square with transparent plastic edges works well.

Get a square the length of the long edge of your drawing board. Buy the best quality you can afford, but avoid fancy versions. They can look great, but may not perform as well as the standard model with an AM radio and blackwall tires.

People who do a lot of drafting frequently use a *drafting machine*, which combines the functions of a T-square, triangles, and architect's scale. This machine does not do the drafting for you, but is an arrangement of counterbalanced metal rods arranged like a human arm. The pivoted top clamps to the drawing board top

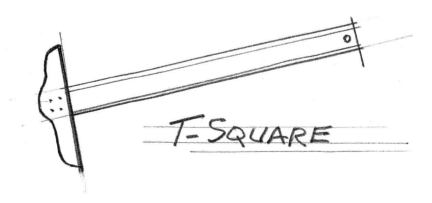

and the head features a knurled knob, which controls two transparent architect's scales at right angles to each other. The knob can turn the scales to any angle, which eliminates the need for the T-square and an array of plastic triangles. Spring tension holds the scales at any position on the drawing board, even when the board is in a near vertical position.

T-Square Don'ts

Don't do any of the following:

- Use it for a hammer
- Cut along its edges
- Allow it to fall on its head
- Let it get wet
- Leave it in the sun
- Let kids play with it
- Loan it to anyone

ARCHITECT'S SCALE

If we were to make drawings in a 1' to 1' scale, our drawings would be as large as the set itself, so someone invented the architect's scale. With this scale, you can convert full-size foot-and-inch measurements into smaller units that represent feet and inches. Be sure to get an *architect's* scale; not an *engineer's* scale which uses a different system. Scales come in different shapes and sizes. The triangular style has two scale systems on each of its three edges. Flat scales have two systems on each of their two edges, and come in short and long sizes. The short model is easy to carry and looks very professional sticking out of your pocket, but the longer sizes are better for drafting board use. Most construction drawings for film and video use ¼" equals 1' and ½ " equals 1' scale.

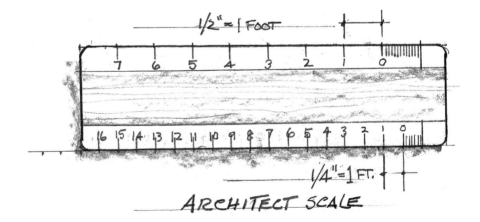

ARCHITECT SCALE

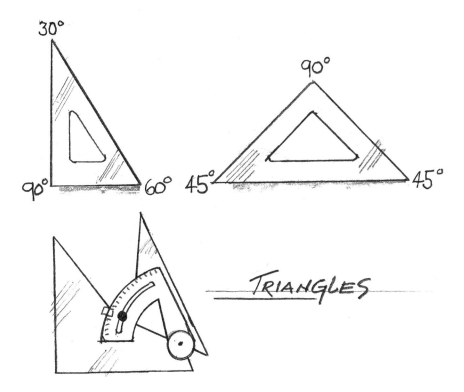

The same **don'ts** apply to architect's scales as those listed for T-squares, plus don't draw lines against the edges. This bad practice can spoil the accuracy of the tiny marks. Above all, don't hurl the scale across the room when things go wrong.

TRIANGLES

These useful pieces of transparent plastic have three perfectly straight edges placed at different angles to each other. When a triangle is placed on your paper with one edge snugged against the T-square edge, you can draw vertical lines and lines at angles. A 30-60-90-degree triangle has three corners available for drawing those angles. The same system applies to a 45-45-90-degree triangle. An adjustable triangle allows you to draw any angle.

YOUR WORK AREA

You need a place to work. This does not mean that you need a big studio with skylights. Dream about that for the future. The corner of a room with a drawing board, stool, lamp, and a small chest of drawers in which to keep the stuff we've been talking about works well.

If you have not splurged on a pedestal or legged drawing board, be creative. Support your board at an angle on a table; use stacked boxes for storage; and fasten a piece of soft composition board to the wall for pinning up drawings and ideas. Pushpins work well here, but not on your drawing board.

COMPUTER-AIDED DRAFTING

A basic computer-aided drafting (CAD) system requires a powerful computer with plenty of memory and hard disk space, CAD software, and a plotter that can make large prints.

Some studios that produce daily shows such as daytime dramas and game shows, have found the CAD system useful, because it allows rapid day-to-day set drawing changes without hand redrafting or using overlays to make prints. However, designers familiar with the CAD system have to make the changes.

If you want to consider buying a system, find someone who uses one on a daily basis, and see what they have to say about its practicality for individual designers.

•

With sketches and basic tools at hand, let's go on to the next chapter and begin the construction drawings.

13

THE CONSTRUCTION DRAWINGS

Now that you have done the research, the producer and director have approved the sketches, and your drawing board and tools are ready, the next step is to translate the sketches into working drawings for the construction shop.

TYPES OF CONSTRUCTION DRAWINGS

Film and video drafting differs from other types. Engineering and architectural drafting require precise detail, because the products made from these types of drawings have to last a long time and are manufactured to close tolerances. Film and video drafting, however, uses many standard units, such as flats, platforms, and backings, and displays mostly surfaces instead of internal structure. Engineers and architects are horrified by what appears to be sloppy work on set construction prints, but such prints are standard to set carpenters who are not concerned with close tolerances.

This is not to say that your drawings can be sloppy, but that they should show as much precision and detail as necessary, based on standard set-construction practice. For example, you need not draw the backs of flats because set carpenters know how they should look.

Shops need specific information to determine material and labor charges. If you work for a producer who does not have studio construction facilities available, print several sets of your construction drawings for shop bids.

If you work at a studio with a construction shop, your drawings will be reviewed by an estimator to determine costs. If you have designed a set that exceeds the cost estimated in the budget, simplify the design by cutting down on the amount of detailing or changing the size of units, unless you can talk the producer into allowing more money.

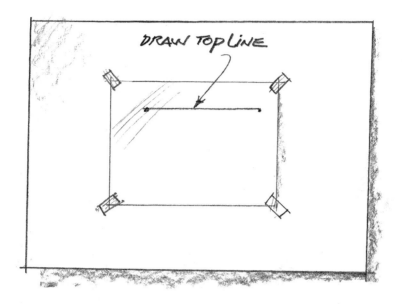

The Plan View

Begin with temporary drawings, which you will arrange under the full sheet tracing paper in the last step. Draw a *temporary* plan view of Patty's living room. The *plan view* shows the set from the top with no perspective. Look at your sketch and decide how wide the upstage wall should be. Remember that sets usually look larger on camera than they do to the eye. Measure a familiar room for comparison.

Tape a 12" x 14" piece of tracing paper to your drawing board. With your T-square head snugly against the left edge of the drawing board (if you are right-handed), slide the square in place with your left hand and draw a light line across the paper about two inches from the top. With the 1/2" equals 1'side of your architect's scale on the light line, make a dot at the 0-feet mark and another dot at the number you have determined will be the width of the upstage living room wall

Draw the right and left walls by the same method – T-square, light line, architect's scale, dots, and heavy line – using a vertical triangle edge with the right-angle edge against the T-square.

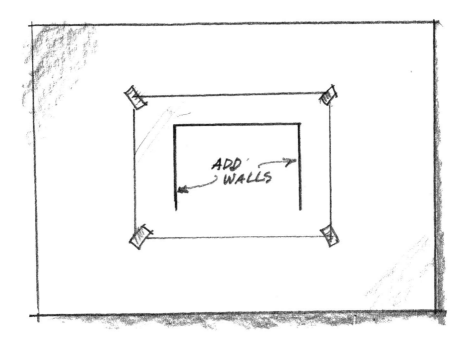

Furnish the Room

Indicate some major pieces of furniture (as seen from above) if you wish, just to see how these objects fit into the set, but draw them to scale also. Art supply stores stock templates with shapes representing tables, chairs, sofas, and kitchen appliances in various scales.

You have now finished the temporary plan view of Patty's living room, but without any dimension numbers or lines that you will add on the full sheet drawing. For the present, leave this temporary drawing simple, without adding windows and doors, because those will go on the full sheet.

The Elevation Views

The plan view shows the set from the top with no perspective. Now draw three temporary *elevation views* — just the outlines that show the walls as though you are standing in front of them. By now you are familiar with your trusty T-square, triangles, and architect's scale, so make individual (from the front) views of the left wall, back wall, and right wall. Show the walls ten feet high and the same width of the walls shown on the plan view.

THE NEXT STEP

With your T-square as a guide, line up the three elevation drawings in the top third of your drawing board about three inches apart. Place the *plan* drawing a couple of inches below the left wall elevation drawing, and tape all in place.

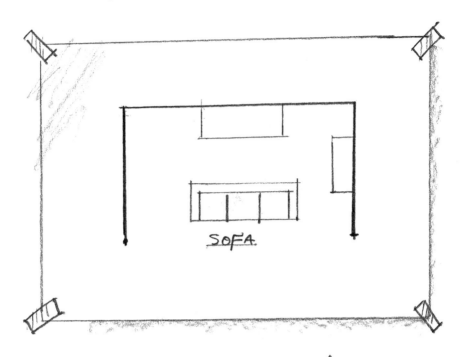

PLAN VIEW

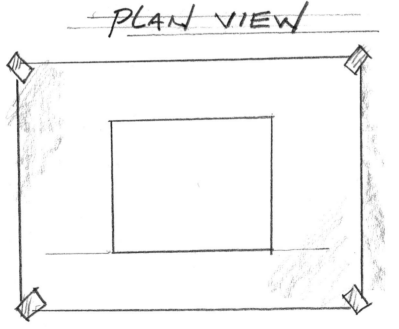

ELEVATION DRAWING
MAKE ③ — RIGHT WALL, BACKWALL
AND LEFT WALL

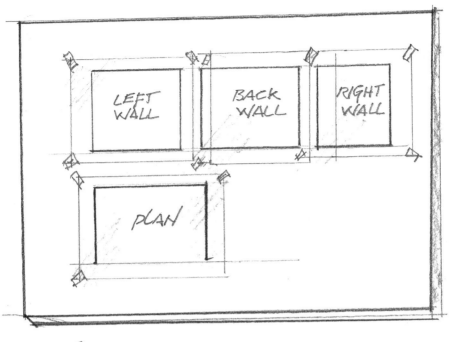

TAPE DRAWINGS TO BOARD

Transfer Temporary Drawings

Tear off a piece of tracing paper large enough to cover all the temporary drawings and tape it in place at the corners. Allow room around the edges of the large piece of paper to draw borders and a title block at the bottom right corner. Trace the outlines of the temporary drawings on the large paper.

●

Now you have the foundation for the construction drawing. In the next chapter, we will add dimension lines, numbers, and the rest of the building information.

14

FINISHING THE CONSTRUCTION DRAWINGS

One of the most satisfying aspects of the art director's job is to see the dressed and lit sets standing on the stage. Before this can happen though, the next step is to finish the drawings.

TRANSFER THE DRAWINGS

What you should have now is a row of three elevation drawings of Patty's living room at the top of your large sheet of tracing paper, and a plan view of the room at the lower left, with a generous amount of blank space around the edges of the drawing sheet.

Now that you have traced the major outlines, remove the individual temporary drawings from under the large sheet. Save the temporary drawings just in case.

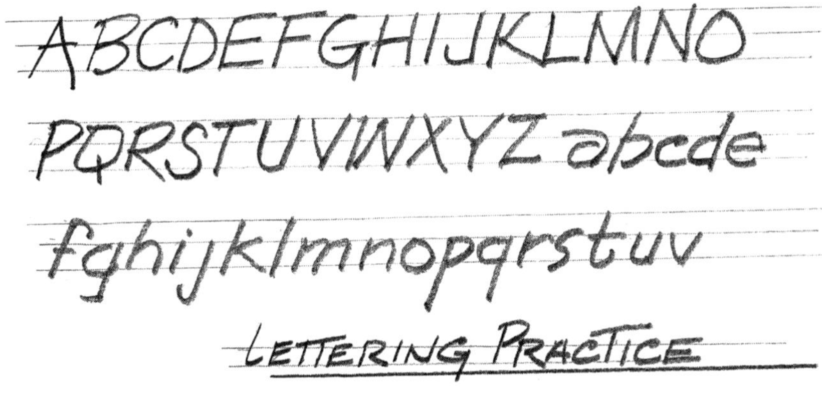

ABCDEFGHIJKLMNO

PQRSTUVWXYZ abcde

fghijklmnopqrstuv

LETTERING PRACTICE

During the tracing process, some of the pencil lines from the surfaces of the individual drawings may have transferred themselves to the back of the large sheet. Turn the large sheet over, erase the unwanted lines, and tape the sheet back to your drawing board.

Lettering

Soon you will need to do some lettering. Practice by drawing three light guidelines on a piece of paper, and fill some practice sheets. If you have a lot of difficulty at first, buy a lettering template. As your skill improves, you will develop your own style without the template.

Line Weights

Use three line weights (thicknesses): *heavy* for the outlines of the flats, *medium* for the lettering and stagefloor line, and *light* for the dimension lines. Practice drawing the three types of lines on another sheet of paper until you can produce lines that are clearly different from one another. Remember that *very* light lines will not reproduce well in the blueprinting process.

Draw a medium-weight, continuous line across the bottom of the three elevation views. Letter "Stage Floor" just below the line to show that the flats will stand on the stage floor and are not suspended above it.

HEAVY

MEDIUM

LIGHT

LINE WEIGHTS

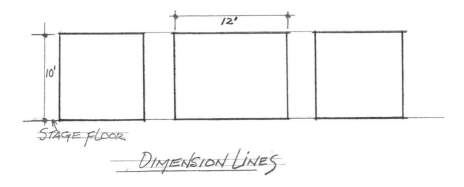

Begin drawing *dimension* lines with your lightweight line far enough away from the heavy outline to leave room for the height or width numbers. If the flats are all the same height, just draw the dimension line once. Indicate the ends of dimension lines with a light horizontal or vertical line and a dot or small slash where the lines cross. This little end line should not touch the outline, because carpenters may think it is a line to build.

Letter in the numbers showing the flat heights and widths. Make the numbers clear so that they stand out from the weight of the dimension lines. When you have finished the dimension lines and numbers, stand back from the drawing and see if the flat outlines stand out clearly. If not, make the outlines bolder.

Begin Labeling the Flats

About an inch below the stagefloor line, draw light guidelines below the row of elevation drawings. On this line and centered below each of the three wall flats, draw a 1/2"-diameter circle with a circle template or compass. On the plan drawing, draw the same size circle about a half inch away from the inside of the wall lines and draw an arrow around the circle pointing at the wall line.

Beginning with the left-side flat elevation drawing, put a letter A inside the circle, a B inside the middle flat circle, and a C inside the right flat circle, and the word "Elevation." Put the corresponding letter inside the circle-arrows on the plan view. Now, no one will have any trouble seeing which flat is which on both views.

LOOK AT THE DETAILS

At this point, the drawing only shows flat surfaces with dimension lines. Begin the fun part by adding elements that will give the drawing interest and life—paneled doors, door frame moldings, wall-surface treatments, windows, baseboards, and light switches. Long unbroken wall surfaces can be uninteresting unless you have a reason to make them so. Break the monotony by adding jogs in the walls. Also, when the wall run is long, it will be constructed of several pieces, which means

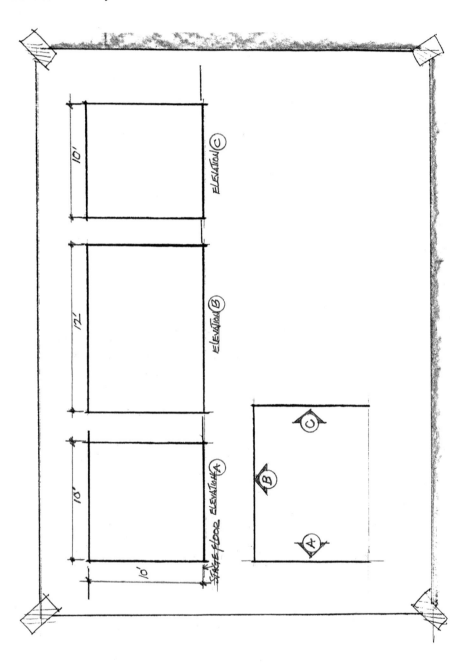

there will be joints to cover. If the wall has a textured surface, the irregularities won't show, but try using short flats *planted on* (covering) over the joints or on long wall runs. Remember that the cameras will see only portions of the set in most shots, so long blank sections may look awkward. Indicate wall-surface treatments

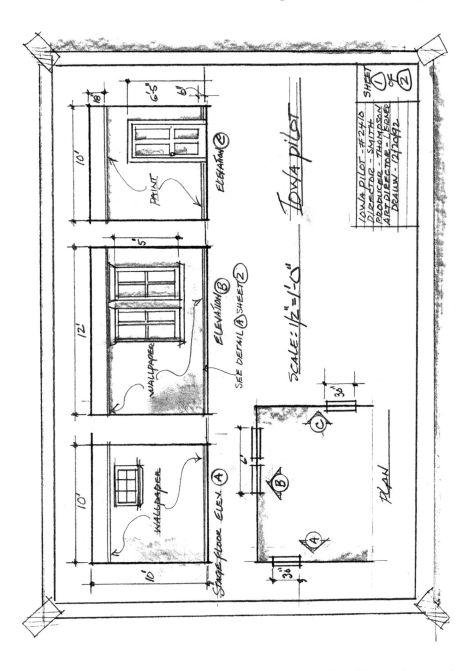

on the elevation views. Show wallpaper pattern and paint-chip numbers and relevant information for the scenic artists who will paint the set. Provide paint-chip samples for the painters, and indicate the amount of day-to-day wear the set should reveal by showing the amount of aging: light, medium, or heavy. Detail drawings of complex moldings or other architectural features may be too small to clearly explain on a ½"- or ¼"-scale construction drawing. Indicate these by lettering "Detail A on sheet 2" with an arrow showing where the piece occurs and make a construction drawing in larger scale on another drawing sheet with appropriate labels.

If you are using some *stock flats* or already-built units, indicate them on the elevation and plan drawings. Be sure they will fit your plan by taking accurate measurements before you draw them to scale.

Finishing Touches

Boldly letter the word "PLAN" below the plan view, and "ELEVATIONS" below the elevation views. Near the bottom of the sheet, letter "SCALE – 1/2" = 1' or whatever scale you are using. Draw a heavy line around the edges of the sheet about 1" in from the borders.

At the lower right corner of the border, draw a *title block* about 3 inches high by 5 inches wide with lines containing basic information: production title and number, set name, producer, director, art director, shooting dates, drawing scale, drawing date, approved by, budget number, sheet number, draftsperson, and total number of sheets. Whew! Lots of information, but useful and necessary.

OFF TO THE BLUEPRINTER

Before you have the construction drawings printed, go over them with the director, the producer, and any other concerned people. Remember that many staff members have trouble interpreting construction drawings, so have the set sketch at hand to help explain. Try to avoid making major changes at this point. If you have to make alterations, be glad you did the drawings in pencil.

Blueprinting (all prints used to be blue) is the traditional, practical way to make many copies of drawings done on tracing paper. The print machine passes the tracing under lights that expose sensitized paper which is then developed by chemical fumes. Most shops can make prints with black, brown, or blue lines.

Print your first set with black lines. Then, if you have to make changes on the tracing sheet, have the second set printed in blue, and any successive sets in alternating colors. This makes it easier to distinguish changes to successive sets of prints. Call attention to changes by drawing a clear arrow with the word "CHANGE" and the date at the changed portion. If you do not want to change your original tracing sheet, the printer can produce a brown-line copy on translucent paper, from which you can chemically erase lines, draw new ones, and have new regular prints made.

Give the construction shop as many sets of prints as they request, and distribute other sets to the company staff — producer, director, production manager, crew chief, lighting director, director of photography, technical director, assistant director, prop master, and stage manager. In other words, everyone who needs to know what is going on.

●

When the construction drawings are finished and printed, you can easily make a simple model of the set, using prints. The next chapter shows how to make this helpful aid.

15

MODEL MAKING

Models communicate space, size, and shape to company members who are not familiar with interpreting sketches and construction drawings. Models also help the art director see the set more clearly and make changes that could be expensive once the sets are built. This chapter tells you how to make a simple set model using construction prints.

DIFFERENT TYPES OF MODELS

Models depicting theatrical and architectural structures are usually more detailed than those made for film and video work. A theatrical set model may even have a miniature built-in lighting system to show lighting changes. Architectural models usually contain more detail and show interior structure because architects are concerned with structural engineering. Film and video models commonly show mostly surfaces because those are what the camera sees, not what holds up the set.

OUR WHITE SET

We are going to see how to build a simple *white* model — no color — the purpose of which is to show the scale of the walls, proportions of spaces, and the location of openings. Later, you may want to make models that show color. If so, color the pieces before you put the model together.

First, for any model, determine the scale you wish to use. Our example uses construction prints that we have drawn using a ½" equals 1' scale. If you want to use a different scale for a model not using prints, remember that you will have to make new drawings to accommodate the different scale.

MAKING THE MODEL

You will need the following materials before you are ready to make a model:

- Plan and elevation prints
- Metal T-square and triangle
- Drafting tape
- Cutting knife such as an X-acto

GLUE plan TO BASE

- Mat board, tag board, or plastic foam-based board – thick and thin
- Glue of your choice
- Pins – glass-head or pushpins
- Wood – Balsa strips and flat sheets
- Paint, colored pencils, markers (if you wish to color the model)

Start with a Sound Base

Thick foam-based board – a sandwich of two thin sheets of paper or plastic with a core of foam plastic – is rigid and light; a good base material. Use thin sheets of the same material for walls and some details. Mat board, thick paper, tag board, and thin balsa sheets are good wall materials and are easy to cut with a mat knife.

Slicing and Gluing

Cut two pieces of foam board: one plan-view size heavier piece for the model base, and one elevation-size thinner piece for the walls. Always cut *away* from your body and use your *metal* T-square or straightedge and a *metal* triangle. *Never* cut against any of your wood or plastic-edged tools! Spray glue or rubber cement the plan-view print to the piece of heavier foam board. Leave three inches of space outside the wall lines if you want to place backings outside the windows and doors. Leave room for a title and other information at the lower right corner.

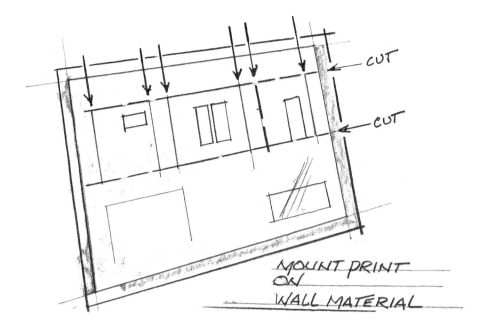

MOUNT PRINT
ON
WALL MATERIAL

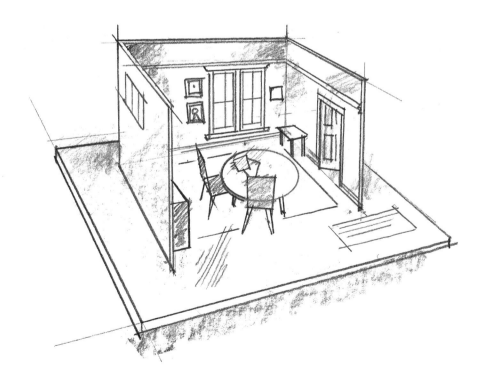

Cement the elevation-view print to the lighter piece of foam board or other thin wall material you've chosen and cut the wall views out. With *dots* of glue, fasten the walls in position on the plan-view base. If you use a lot of glue, the model will be difficult to change later if necessary. If you prefer, you can tape the joints on the back of the corners.

SHOWING THE MODEL

To help model viewers visualize the size of the set, place a simple stylized scale human figure in or near the model as you did on the sketches. To enhance the model's realism, visit a model shop that stocks scale-model furniture, wallpaper, and bric-a-brac, or make your own from balsa wood. The figure below shows the completed model with title block in the front right corner, which finishes the presentation. When exhibiting your model to those concerned, encourage them to hold the model at eye level, which will give them a better impression of available camera angles. If you must make changes, remember that you have saved the original tracings and can make changes for new prints to use for both construction drawings and a model.

•

The sketches, construction drawings, and model have laid the groundwork for the finished set. In the next chapter, we will see that the art director still has a lot to do when supervising construction, stage setup, and set dressing.

16

SUPERVISING CONSTRUCTION AND SETUP

When the construction drawings and model are finished and approved, the art director finds a construction shop to build the sets, supervises construction, and oversees the stage setup. Production designer Colin Irwin describes his supervision process:

> If there's an art director working under me, a lot of the supervision is his job. The set designer is only on to do the drawings. The art director deals with the everyday jobs because I am busy doing other things. Once I have approved the drawings and send them to the shop, I just pop in once in a while and look at the finishes on the walls. I want to see what the camera will see. On the first shoot day, I open the set with the set decorator and stay until the first shot is done. There's an on-set dresser who moves furniture around and works with the prop department. Unless there's a special reason to have an art director on the set, I don't usually do that because there's not the time or the money.

GETTING BIDS

If the studio selected by the producer has a construction shop, the sets may be built on the lot as part of the production agreement. If not, the art director takes the construction drawings to several shops for bids. The lowest bid is not necessarily the best one because a shop may want the job badly enough to cut corners, to the detriment of the job. Besides price, the art director considers the quality of their work and the reliability of each shop.

The entire set may not have to be built new. Shops usually store stock flats and units used in previous productions. Major production centers have independent rental warehouses that rent used pieces such as fireplaces and door and window units. The art director compares the rental fee, transportation costs, and refinishing to the cost of new construction.

CONSTRUCTION AND SETUP SUPERVISION

During set construction, the art director or an assistant should monitor progress with an early morning stop at the construction shop and should be available by beeper, phone, or answering machine. The most carefully done construction drawings cannot include all the information that may be needed.

The production schedule allows a specified amount of stage setup time. The art director has given the head of the stage crew and carpenters sets of plans showing where the set or sets go on the stage, and monitors the setup. Do the walls fit together properly? Are details, such as moldings, chair rails, and ceiling pieces, placed and finished according to the plans? Have the scenic artists and painters followed the painting plan? Is the set decoration and furnishing appropriate to the setting?

Sometimes the production designer's agreement does not allow supervision during the entire shooting schedule, but usually the production designer is responsible for supervision and design work for the duration of the shoot.

A typical property rental house

SET DECORATION

The set decorator, working with plans and suggestions provided by the art director, locates and rents or purchases furniture, drapery, and decorative accessories. This person also keeps a running account of costs.

Production designer Larry Miller describes his working relationship with a set decorator:

> I always come up with a color concept to guide the decorator. The decorator I have used on the last four or five films is wonderful because she is able to go out on her own and if something is not so great, she has no attachment and says, "OK, let's find something else." This is a good quality and not so easy to find.

Major production centers have many prop (property) rental houses that rent furniture and accessories from many periods and in many styles. Most of the rental houses specialize in specific time periods or locales such as western, traditional, colonial, or contemporary.

After studying the script and conferring with the art director, the set decorator roams through property rental houses and selects objects to rent and buys other properties that cannot be rented. The set decorator is also responsible for seeing that the rented and purchased properties arrive at the production stage, and that they are arranged in the set as planned.

Rental charges average about 15 percent per week of the assigned value of each piece. Unless the production company sets up an account with the rental house, the house can require a cashier's check to cover the assigned value of the rented pieces, and another check equal to the rental charge. When the rented props are returned in good condition, the deposit check is returned to the company. The production company must pay for damage to the house's properties. If the production has a long run, prop houses will work out a production rental plan at less cost than weekly rentals.

THE PROP MASTER

Actors use many hand props such as beverage containers, dinnerware, books, and tools. The prop (property) master obtains and cares for these pieces. If the set contains especially valuable pieces, the prop master photographs or marks their positions and stores them in a secure place. Many prop masters own large closets on wheels that contain thousands of objects which may not be planned for but can save the day in an emergency.

The production designer creates special props, such as a telling element in a Steve Martin film:

> In *L.A. Story*, we shot in a lot of restaurants. I love menus and there's a sequence where the maitre d' and the chef interview Steve Martin at the bank to be sure he has the financial depth to get a reservation at their restaurant! The menu is featured in the event, so the menu was BIG and we made up the most pretentious dishes you can imagine!

KEEPING RECORDS

As the set stands from day to day, furniture and other objects must remain in the same place, unless the script requires otherwise, so that shots will match. The set decorator and property master take photographs at the end of each shooting day so that if someone moves objects, the prop master can determine their correct places the next day.

These photographs are extremely valuable if the set has been struck (dismantled) and has to be reset for more photography. Photographs also enhance the set decorator's sample book. Standard practice is to place a rope or other barrier across the set with a sign "Hot Set" to let everyone know that the set is not to be disturbed. The set decorator also keeps copies of the property rental house's invoices listing the objects that can be rented again for additional setups.

THE CRITIQUE

We can see that the art director's job is not finished when the sets have been designed. The production designer and art director take a hard look at the sets when they are standing, lit, and dressed, and compares the result with the beginning concept.

Maybe the living room was too large, as the director predicted, or the nightclub wasn't grand enough. Perhaps the backing behind a window wasn't convincing because the haze generator didn't work. Ah well! There's always the next time.

•

So far, we have seen the technical and the creative demands made on an art director. Now, in Part III, we will see more about what the range of an art director's work is like when production gets underway on some typical projects.

Part III

TYPICAL SETS
AND OPPORTUNITIES

A designer meets many different challenges. This part details several typical ones: location work, a talk show, a news broadcasting environment, and a commercial, with emphasis on creating innovative designs.

For the novice considering an art direction career, the last chapter offers suggestions on allied fields in which to gain applicable experience, as well as how to prepare a résumé and portfolio and where to look for a position in television or film.

17

A PRODUCTION DESIGNER ON LOCATION

Leaving the convenience of the stage to work on location presents a different set of requirements for the art director, as well as for the rest of the crew. The art director and crew must carefully document the location scene, because they will have to make some of the stage work match.

Colin Irwin, art director on the film *JFK*, describes some work done to make a location in Dallas, Texas, match documentary film footage used in the movie:

> We did a lot of adding to locations, but not much building. We rented the oval office set from Paramount. In Daly Plaza we added to and changed it to match the 8mm film footage used in the movie. We had to trim the trees back, move signs and lampposts, and bring in 10 or 12 truckloads of dirt to cover the concrete parking lot. We also put in styrofoam railroad tracks as the original metal ones were no longer there.

The distance factor is a major consideration for the producer. A location may require minutes to days of travel, and unknown and unpredictable factors can be expensive and time-consuming.

PATTY'S TOWN MOVES

A television network has funded one filmed pilot episode of the Iowa drama. Our producer hopes network programmers will be so enchanted with the result that they will order six more episodes, that the series will run for more than one season, and that it will become a syndicated product.

The producer decides to film all the interiors and the park scene on stage and to find a nearby small town that can be used, with some alterations, for exteriors. The producer and director do not feel that existing movie-lot exterior sets are convincing enough for the mood of the story.

Marian Lerner, who specializes in location work, has signed on as art director. She has contracted for six weeks' work and has received a check from the company for one-third of her total fee, the other portions of which are scheduled to appear at two-week intervals. After presenting sketches, models, and construction drawings, Marian is ready to go on a location-survey trip.

Marian's research tells her a lot about the kind of town they are seeking, so she gets information on nearby small towns from the state motion picture office. She confers with the producer and production manager and they decide to look at two towns: Clarion and Two Forks. Both are in flat country and have stores and houses of adaptable style.

They drive to Clarion to see the town and countryside. The landscape is indeed flat, as the film office said, but they didn't mention the range of hills in the distance. Marian sees that while Clarion's main street has some older buildings, suitable with some alterations for the flashback scenes, present-day merchants have done complete refacings and erected big signs – complicated and expensive to remove.

Meeting the Mayor and Documenting a Location

The group meets with the mayor, who is eager to see the town on television – it would be good for business. The producer makes it clear that they are considering other towns and that their decision will be based on many factors, although Clarion is a fine-looking place.

Marian gets a street map of Clarion and takes many photographs of Main Street, individual buildings, the newspaper office, and residences. She places a yardstick, marked off at one-foot intervals with white tape, in each photograph so that if she needs to make scale drawings of the buildings, the size of the buildings will be apparent.

Down the Road a Piece and Back

The crew drives a few miles down the road to Two Forks. While this town is similar in appearance to Clarion, it does not have adequate lodging facilities for the cast and crew. Also, its main street features many palm trees, which are rarely found in Iowa, in the Main Street's center divider – a problem for aerial establishing shots. Also, the mayor is not eager to see his town overrun with "movie people" in spite of increased income for merchants. As no other likely looking towns been located, the producer chooses Clarion.

The survey group returns to their base and the production manager prepares letters of agreement and contracts for individuals and businesses that will be involved in the production, and returns to Clarion a few days later to get the required permits from the mayor's office.

Marian and George, the assistant art director, go back to Clarion for some more preproduction work. They visit the newspaper office and explain that during the production they will need to fasten a temporary sign over the existing sign on the outside of the building. The new sign will arrive with the shop-built scenery and props a few days before the first day of shooting.

How About Dusty Rose, Mrs. Jones?

The design crew visits Mrs. Jones's house, which will represent the exterior of script character Patty's residence. The efficient production manager has arranged, with Mrs. Jones's permission, to repaint the front of her house, which currently is an unsuitable color combination for Patty's character. Marian explains that if Mrs. Jones wishes, after the shoot finishes, they will repaint her house in the original colors. Mrs. Jones says that she will wait and see how she likes the new paint job.

Marian and George scrutinize the business and street signs in the areas to be seen on camera and photograph the ones that will need to be replaced or covered. They also notice that a tree to be seen in the shots covering the outside of the newspaper office is a southern climate tree that will need some masking foliage appropriate to Iowa.

The Union

Because the pilot episode will be made under union rules, the basic crew will be taken to the location and laborers and some assistants will be hired in Clarion. If Clarion had its own union locals, the local office would provide all the working personnel.

OFF TO LOCATION

Two weeks later, when the construction shop is building the stage production sets, Marian and George pack their location survival kits: comfortable shoes, rain clothes, cameras, and basic drawing supplies, as well as changes of clothes and personal necessities. Living in a motel can be a dreary experience, but because the art staff usually spends the major part of the day and evening running around solving problems, they won't spend much time in their rooms staring at the bad paintings screwed to the walls.

Winter at Six A.M.

Marian and George arrive in Clarion two days before the first shoot day. The new signs and props have arrived by truck. They supervise sign installations, the repainting of Mrs. Jones's house, and the disguise of the tree in front of the newspaper office — all observed by fascinated town residents who ask many questions. Marian and George meet with the locally hired helpers and provide them with schedules for each of the shoot days, as well as meal vouchers redeemable at a local restaurant.

On the first day, Marian meets George and their crew in the motel lobby at six A.M. The crew consists of a head prop person, assistant prop person, a truck driver, and four greenspeople who will make the Jones house and yard area look as if it's winter. Marian goes over the day's schedule, which includes the first setup in front of the newspaper office, and after lunch, winter at the Jones house.

Art directors on location try to think of everything they need to take with them, but frequently they have to do their own legwork. Set decorator and art director Robert Cecchi recalls this about another location shoot:

> I was doing a western in Arizona and I asked a local guy where I could get some kerosene. He gave me a blank stare and said he didn't know, but I found a hardware store and bought it there. The same with lamp chimneys. Locals should know where to get anything, but I had to go out and waste my time.

The Shoot Continues

Marian sends the greenspeople to the house and she, George, and an assistant go to the newspaper exterior location. They supervise the tree foliage alteration, and the cast and crew are ready to begin the first shot of the day. The actor playing Patty's role will park her car in front, get out of the car, and enter the office front door. An assistant director in charge of atmosphere will see that cars move down the street and local extras hurry down the sidewalk. Marian looks at the video monitor, which shows what the film camera sees, and notices that some of the natural unwanted tree leaves show in the shot. She asks a crew member to move more of the artificial branches to cover the leaves.

To deal with problems that come up during the morning, George stays with the company, and Marian goes to the Jones house to supervise winter. Marian has the crew spray more snow on the porch roof and frost the side windows that will show in an angle shot. The crew has turned a leafed-out summer shrub into a snowman and is snowing the lawn.

The company arrives after lunch. By six P.M., when the light has changed too much to continue day scenes, everyone goes to dinner, only to come back to the house for night scenes. Marian and George have to spend much time during the day waiting for the next camera setup, and preparing the set for the next setup.

After dinner and the night scenes finish, Marian and George meet with their crew and go over the next day's schedule. George collects receipts for cash he has given them during the day for emergency items. The production manager gives George cash, for which he must account, and also has to set up a drawing account at the local bank for the art crew. When George returns to the motel at the end of each day, he balances the receipts and cash, and places them in an envelope.

It's ten P.M. and all has gone well except for a noisy aircraft and a balky camera. George sets his alarm for five-thirty A.M. and turns on the television news. There they are at Mrs. Jones's winterized house as a reporter in summer clothes exclaims over the wonder of it all. Clarion is already famous!

BACK TO THE CITY AGAIN

When the location work wraps, Marian and George return to their familiar haunt, the soundstage, and supervise the setup, set decoration, and daily shooting process. Because the producer wants a realistic view of production problems if the network buys six more episodes (the producer hopes), the company takes one week to shoot the pilot episode. This procedure gives Marian and George time to evaluate what their work will be like on a weekly basis.

Deborah Lakeman, an experienced weekly series set decorator, describes the process on a typical production:

Ideally, we have a script on Monday, but that gets totally rewritten by Tuesday. There's a production meeting just to talk about what's going on that week and maybe the next so you can get a head start. We try to be a week or two ahead.

I read the script and make lists of what I will need to find, discussing it with the art director, who gives me samples of the wall colors. Most of the time I have a budget to work with, but it's not always realistic. We sometimes choose the colors together.

With the list, I go to the prop houses and take Polaroid shots of the pieces I want to use and the prop house puts a tag on each piece to hold it for our show. I then show the pictures to the art director, director, producers, and sometimes the star. A lot of times, the producers and star will base a choice on their own personal taste or what they have at home instead of what is appropriate for the characters. After the decisions are made, I have a truck pick up the rental pieces and bring them to the stage where the crew puts them in place.

If we are a week ahead, I can combine working on two episodes at once. I have a beeper and a phone in my car, because as the director and actors get into the set, changes start happening. The set is never finished. Rewrites happen every day.

As Deborah Lakeman said, sometimes actors' wishes influence her job, but Robert Cecchi reports that their frailties can influence a set decorator's job too:

When I worked on a film starring Barbara Stanwyck, I always had to provide her with something to lean on. She was in her seventies and the ludicrous thing was that her character was supposed to be having a love affair with a rodeo rider! On another job, we were working in an airport control tower and one of the actors couldn't remember his lines, so someone wrote them on pieces of paper and I arranged the set so that the action could be staged with the actor always behind a computer terminal or some piece of equipment where the papers could be placed within his sight.

Either George or Marian is present each shooting day to make sure that all is well with the set and to take care of unexpected changes. When they view the footage at the postproduction house where the program is edited, they ignore the dialogue and watch the pictures, focusing their attention on the work they did to alter the small-town environment, of course. If the sign over the newspaper office door had been a little lower, it would have established itself better. They also notice that the snow cover outside the house did not quite obscure some grass at the bottom of the frame, but because this was a night shot, a cast shadow covered the error. George is glad he took pictures of the frost on the front windows of the Jones house so they can duplicate the pattern on the stage set windows. As a whole, however, George and Marian felt their work was convincing to the camera.

●

Many art directors prefer to do location work, because it presents challenges and opportunities for improvisation, miles from nowhere. In the next chapters, we will see what an innovative art director can do with commonplace design problems.

18

STAGING A TALK SHOW

The art director plays a major role in the presentation of a talk show. In the preceding chapter's example of a drama taking place in a small town, the art director's job was to analyze the characters and their environments, to help create the mood for the drama, and to provide the physical requirements of the action. Other types of productions, however, offer few visual clues. What forms, colors, and textures will define the space, satisfy the practical requirements, and project a mood?

Don Merton, an experienced video art director, describes some typical problems for the designer:

> Many times they say they want something different, but when it comes down to it, they want to play it safe. That's why the talk shows all look the same. You can hardly tell one from another. It's true that the requirements are similar—a desk, a host, and an audience—but I always try to get them to do something different. Usually I can go just so far.

THE PRODUCTION MEETING

The producer of our talk show tells us that the host is a warm, friendly person, and that the mood of the show is to be casual and relaxed. We have some character definition and mood to work with, even though this is not a drama.

Right away, some obvious set solutions come to mind. How about the L-shaped couch, a coffee table with a plant, and bookcase walls with a fireplace? Well, that's always acceptable and easy to shoot, and all we have to do is drag out a set of drawings made three years ago. The producer, however, has had that one pulled on her before, and she is an expert cliché-spotter.

She says, "I want to do something different. Just because the host has a friendly act going, I don't want to see him behind a desk next to a couch and coffee table.

I want to see him in a simple set that will allow the cameras to move around the set while they stay invisible. I don't want to pay camera operators fees for on-camera appearances." Here we thought this was going to be Talk Show 1-A and that we could design it between coffee break and lunch.

This Is Going to Mean Real Work

"Tell me more," you say. "You want the cameras to move anywhere while they're invisible?" This producer talks as though she believes we are magicians instead of art directors.

She goes on, "I am looking for an arrangement that will allow the host and guest to be undisturbed by the mechanics of the show. I want them to be able to carry on an absorbing conversation, undistracted by studio activity. The viewer will be an eavesdropper. We're going to fade in on a conversation in progress. The host is not going to turn to the camera and say, 'Hi! I'm Larry Garralous!'"

Well — a different idea at last. The couch, coffee table, and bookcase flats will stay asleep in the warehouse and we will have to put our creative brains in high gear.

To begin to solve the problem we ask, "What are the basic elements?" and discuss how to proceed. Two seated people, hidden cameras, and a background. When two people talk, they usually face each other. If the camera sees them side-by-side, they will be in profile, constantly turning their heads. The cameras have to get straight on to the two faces, but if they do that, are the cameras going to see each other? Yes, they will, but if we set the two people at a slight angle to each other, head-turning will be minimized. Better still, we will figure out a way they can face each other.

THE GREAT CHAIR SEARCH
AND THE PROPER HEIGHT

What kind of chairs? The chairs' design should prevent slouching and make the sitter appear to have good posture. The seats and backs should be firm so that the sitter does not sink in and appear to be part of the upholstery. The backs of chairs should be covered by the sitter so that the sitter does not appear to have sprouted wings, and the chairs' height needs to prevent sprawling.

Upholstered dining armchairs usually look good on camera because they satisfy the requirements. Avoid swivel chairs unless the talent can sit still. When a nervous guest swivels, viewers can become seasick. Avoid using high director's chairs because on wide shots, the occupants appear to be sitting on perches.

Seating on the Upper Platform Only

Because the four cameras to be used on this program will not be mounted on cranes or low dollies and cannot get *down* to the eye levels of the host and guest, the cameras will be forced to look down at the show participants if their chairs are on the stage floor. We will bring the seating up to eye level with a platform.

Platforms do not have to be boring rectangles. Remember that platforms become part of the set design on wide shots, and that they can be an interesting combination of shapes and colors. Depending on the height of the platform, a wide step or steps with at least 12-inch wide treads adds design interest as well as helping guests get up there. Allow at least a 4' x 4' space for each seated person. Instrumental groups require special attention, because different instruments need different amounts of space and, in some cases such as drum sets, special floor treatment.

DIFFERENT APPROACHES

Now that we have taken care of the chair and platform parts of the set, the most difficult problem faces us: the invisible cameras. How are we going to hide them if they are going to freely roam the set? The director, of course, can block the cameras so that they do not see each other, but we can be helpful by figuring out ways to let them hide while allowing the lenses free access.

One way would be to use a black cyclorama all the way around the stage walls and have the cameras using zoom lenses work as far away from the platform area as possible . Using this idea, the cameras might have to be draped in black cloth. This approach, however, will leave our fascinating conversation sitting in a black void.

We can do research for a talk-show set in the same way we did for the Iowa pilot. Architectural and home decoration magazines are full of *forms* and *materials* that, when viewed as abstract shapes, can be developed into set pieces. The three basic shapes — circle, square, and triangle — are the design foundation of everything we see and can be put together in countless ways, as you will see by analyzing architectural designs.

Scrim Shot

In one of the magazines, we see some tall, sheer drapery fabric hanging behind the front windows of a bank building. Because the light level outside the building is higher than that inside the building, the curtains are opaque from the outside and transparent from the inside.

To ape the bank building drapery, we could hang a stretched *scrim* (gauze fabric) from the grid to the stage floor, eight feet or more from the stage walls,

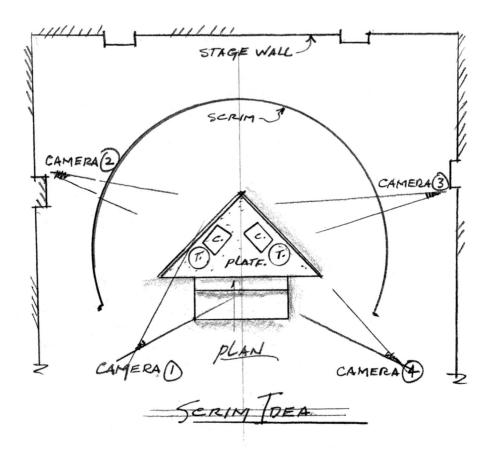

STAGE WALL

SCRIM

CAMERA(2)

CAMERA(3)

C.   C.

T.   T.

PLATE.

CAMERA(1)

CAMERA(4)

PLAN

SCRIM IDEA

going around three sides of the stage. If the scrim is a light color, it will reflect ambient light from the set lighting, or can be patterned with shafts of light, for example. The cameras working behind the scrim will look through the fabric and be hidden from the set side. This approach needs some experimentation to see if the scrim will diffuse the photography too much.

Quick! Draw the Blinds!

Another magazine picture shows some tall, vertical sunlight-control vanes outside a building window. When viewed from one angle, the group of vanes appears to be a solid wall. Another more straight-on view reveals what is beyond the spaces between the blinds. We could design some four-foot-wide vertical flats similar to those in the picture, which would hide the cameras and, from many angles, allow the camera lenses free rein to the set. A simple white model of this design would help the director see this set's possibilities.

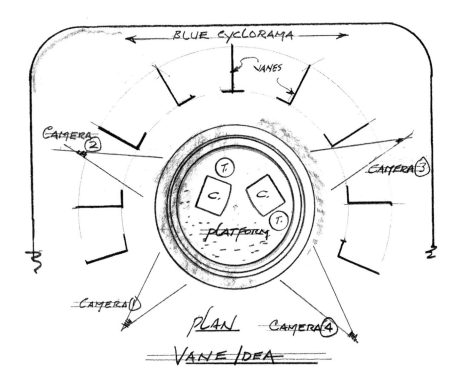

BE IMAGINATIVE!

It's always a pleasure to work with producers and directors who are not willing to settle for obvious solutions, but we must be willing to accept failure too. Maybe a design doesn't work today, but improved technology may let you bring it out of storage later. There are no ideal solutions. All designs have drawbacks, but your choices are unlimited. Good ideas come from unexpected places — we once saw a production designer turn a piece of gutter trash into a planet's surface. Above all, keep your eyes open.

●

Imaginative solutions can be applied to other forms of programming as well. In the next chapter we will see how the art director works out several solutions for a news set and see how they are received.

19

STAGING A NEWS BROADCAST

An independent television station art director recalls the first time he designed a newsroom presentation:

> Way back then, everyone had just a desk and a background. Then someone came up with the bright idea of making the news seem more authentic by showing the whole staff rushing around and there were many problems with this: noise, confusion, and most of the time, nothing happening in the background because by the time the news was on the air, most of the news staff had finished their work!

BACKGROUND ON THE NEWS

News broadcasting is a major source of income for most television stations in the United States and receives a large share of management's attention. In the infancy of television, commercial station news broadcasting played a minor role because viewers wanted to be entertained by the new medium rather than informed. For some people, this is still the case.

Ratings rose when news broadcasters increased news entertainment values and introduced attractive news-reading personalities. Appearance and presentation style became important. The amount of money broadcasters could charge for commercial time increased as audience shares increased. Broadcast lengths increased to allow more time for entertainment and production values. Technological advances enhanced these values.

THE ART DIRECTOR'S ROLE

The appearance and tone of news broadcasts rests heavily on the setting in which viewers see the reporters. The care the art director puts into set design can increase the broadcast's excitement and authority.

Broadcasters place much emphasis on the appearance of the people who talk to the cameras. Many viewers believe that these authoritative-appearing people rush around all day gathering the stories they tell. The reality, however, is that, generally, staffs of reporters, writers, editors, and news-gathering crews prepare the material the on-camera personalities read. An art director contributes one element that helps create an authoritative feeling: the setting.

MAKE IT LOOK LIKE A NEWSROOM!

Let's join a typical production meeting at which a new news presentation will be discussed. The management of WXXX has decided to abandon their traditional broadcast format—three people seated at a curved desk in front of a city photomural. WXXX is going to follow the crowd and do a two-hour newsroom-format program which they hope will win the ratings race in Midland City.

Present at the meeting are the news director, program director, station manager, production manager, technical director, facilities manager, assorted assistants, many coffee cups, and Harold, the art director. After the obligatory chit-chat with which all meetings begin, the station manager says: "I have called this meeting to get the ball rolling on a new secret news show that you all know about. We've been concerned about the success of the newsroom format over at

Channel 8 and in other markets around the country. We're not going to be left behind…(etc., etc.). Now our illustrious news director will tell us about this exciting new project."

The news director starts in. Everyone takes notes. He says the new show will be two hours long, have a newsroom format, and that the news staff will appear in the background doing their regular jobs (which they will have already done by the time the broadcast airs). We hear a lot of enthusiastic talk about how exciting this will be, how we will have new mobile state-of-the-art news-gathering equipment, and the *new look* will make WXXX the highest rated station in the area.

The words "new look" rouse Harold from doodling strange creatures on his yellow pad. New "looks" always mean a set that looks completely different from the old one, but won't scare anybody and has to be ready in two weeks. Harold wonders how exciting he can make a set that contains some editors typing behind a row of news readers.

"When is all this supposed to go on the air?" Harold asks.

"We're shooting for September 8th," says Mr. News Director. A hush falls over the room.

Taking a white-knuckled grip on his coffee cup, Harold says, "That gives me three whole weeks. I don't see how I can design and have a whole new newsroom built by then."

"Don't worry," the news director says. "All we have to do is move the cameras into the old newsroom and put in some lights."

HAROLD GETS BUSY

Harold asks some more questions and returns to his cubicle to begin creating the solution to this new challenge. Setting aside the problems posed by the low ceiling in the existing newsroom, he makes a list of the requirements discussed at the production meeting:

- Anchor desk with four positions
- Chromakey effect (blue or green area for inserting electronic graphics)
- Channel number in every shot
- Clocks showing worldwide times
- Map of the world
- Map of the state
- Bank of television screens

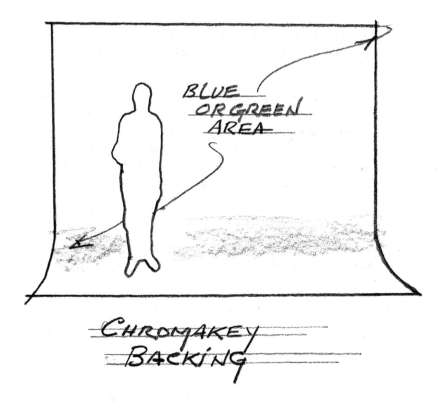

It All Has to Fit

Harold's first job is to record the general dimensions of the room, including the height of the ceiling, changes in floor level, width and height of doors, and jogs in the walls and ceiling. He also measures and counts the desks at which the news-gathering staff will be seen, and makes notes of the positions of computers, television monitors, and telephones he needs to show on the plan.

Back to the Drawing Board

Armed with the numbers, Harold sketches out some ideas. He starts with some obvious solutions and works up to some more innovative plans to present along with the dull ones. He then draws plan views of the room.

Scale It Up

To be sure the new pieces will fit into the existing room, Harold makes scale cardboard shapes representing desks and other necessary furnishings. By trying different arrangements of the shapes, he gets a clearer idea of how the spaces can work. When he has a preliminary arrangement, Harold makes a simple white model of the room. Now the set and its proportions are even more clear because he can hold the model up to camera level and peer at it from any angle.

Don't Forget the Weather

Weather reporting holds extreme interest for many viewers, and Harold reserves a portion of the set for the *Chromakey* process. The weather person stands in front of a blue or green area onto which still and moving graphics are electronically inserted.

The weather reporter looks into an off-camera monitor to see the computer-created graphics. As we saw in Chapter 5, saturated blue and green are the colors of choice because they are far away from the colors reporters usually wear, and allow the system to cut a clear stencil into which the system can insert graphics.

More Numbers

Another item on Harold's list is the channel number appearance desired in every shot of the newsroom so that viewers will not think they are watching Channel 6. At this point in the design process, he has only a rough idea of the camera angles and can only estimate where to put the logos. Harold plans to leave the exact placement until he sees the set on camera and sees the shots chosen by the director.

Clutter Everywhere

Looking at the existing newsroom, Harold sees that it is a visual mess, has no central staff working area, and no color identity. The room serves its purpose as a utilitarian space as determined by the staff's needs, but it will look messy and confusing on camera. Armed with measurements, he decides to make a central anchorperson area toward the end of the room where the cameras will be. This area will be elevated 18" above floor level to get the seated, on-camera people's eyes at lens level. Behind this anchor desk area, the cameras will see feverish news-gathering activity, the wall clocks, and banks of television monitors, as well as a channel number or two. Much of the time, the possibly distracting activity will be out of focus or not in selected shots.

Harold May Scare Them

Because he has several ideas, ranging from ordinary to innovative, Harold makes sketches and rough plans for each. This approach can be risky, because clients may get confused by many choices, but Harold decides the following three designs will give everyone a chance to show their true colors:

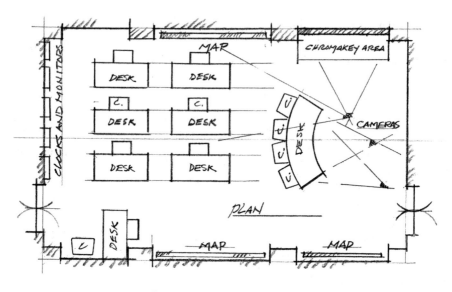

① A STANDARD SOLUTION

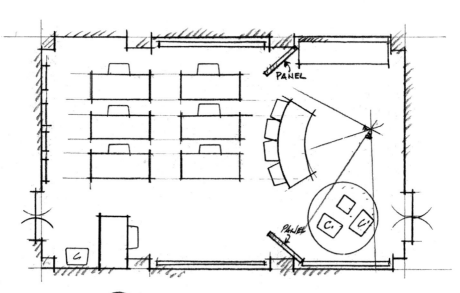

② A DIFFERENT ARRANGEMENT

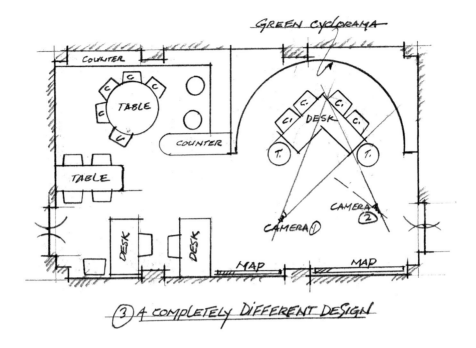

(3) 4 COMPLETELY DIFFERENT DESIGN

1. *A standard solution* — Following the news director's suggestions, Harold places a four-person anchor desk in the foreground, station logo and weather area to the right, and clocks on the wall above. The color tone is beige.
2. *A different arrangement of the same idea* — This version of the set has colored panels, an interview area, and chrome trim around the walls. Everything else is the same as the first plan.
3. *An arrangement that will frighten everyone* — This set has no conventional walls, but features a semi-circular 180° Chromakey green area behind the anchor desk, giving free rein for insertion of news graphics. A curved, transparent desktop at which the news readers sit even shows the bottom half of their figures, a broadcasting innovation.

Ms. Cautious will go for set No. 1 or possibly set No. 2 if she feels daring. Mr. Middle-of-the-Road will not say anything until he hears the station manager's opinion. Mr. Courageous will go for No. 3, whatever may happen to his career.

WHAT'S THE DECISION?

Station management cautiously approaches any changes in news presentation for fear that they may frighten loyal viewers to another channel, so after many hours of soul-searching, they choose to go ahead with Harold's solution No. 2, Middle-of-the Road. Harold files away No. 3 for another day.

●

In the next chapter, we will see how an art director can help present a lot of information in a short period of time by designing a commercial setting.

20

DESIGNING A COMMERCIAL

Besides giving us time to dash to the kitchen for a snack, television commercials support programming that keeps us on the couch in the first place. Jean Carpenter, an art director specializing in commercials, says:

> I like designing commercials because they don't last forever, pay well, and many times offer creative opportunities that don't happen in dramatic work. What I don't like is the need to satisfy so many different elements such as the client's personal opinion which has nothing to do with the finished product. I worked for a producer once who didn't allow the client people on the set! She made that whole group stay in a viewing room and watch production on a monitor!

A commercial's objective is to sell a product, of course. By interviewing consumers and by analyzing sales and demographic data, advertising agencies create messages they hope will cause consumers to buy their product instead of a competitor's. Buyers' choices may not have any bearing on the intrinsic worth of

STORYBOARD PANELS

the product, but can simply be a response to the message and its atmosphere. The art director, then, as a participant in the creation of environments, helps sell products.

STORYBOARDS

What is the difference between an advertising agency art director and a video or film art director? The answer is: An agency art director works with a creative director to create a storyboard and general visual concept for a commercial.

A storyboard is a series of drawings in panels with dialogue or description below each drawing. The video or film art director works from the storyboard and script and creates the sets.

Visual Consultant Bruce Block says:

Storyboards should be simple. They should remind you of the general composition and who's in the shot. They should deal with spatial considerations and line and that's about it. Storyboards should be a work in progress; otherwise, they're comic book illustrations.

COMMERCIAL PRODUCTION PERSONNEL AND PROCEDURES

An advertising agency frequently hires an outside production house to package the production of the commercial. The production house may also hire the set art director.

The advertising agency personnel usually include the following:

- Account executive
- Producer
- Creative director
- Copy writer
- Agency art director

The production house generally provides the following:

- Director
- Art director
- Set decorator
- Food stylist
- Director of photography (DP)
- Stage facility
- Stage crew
- Postproduction services

Dealing with Choices

Differences of opinion affect the commercial art director's job. The client may not like the wallpaper, the set dressing, or the paint color. The producer has the final say and may have to work out compromises; this is another time when the art director needs to be diplomatic.

Daily Labor

The set art director is usually hired to work on a daily basis rather than under a contract agreement. The amount of time available to design and assemble the set elements is generally short, frequently just three or four days. The client, of course, wants to know exactly what the sets are going to look like, so an art director's sketches play a major role and have to be done very quickly.

Labeling and Food

Usually the advertising agency prepares camera-ready labels and special packaging that will photograph better than a store's shelf products. Larger production centers have services that specialize in product labels and packaging, but frequently the prop person or art director handles that part of the job using airbrush, photocopies, and laser prints. If the product is a food item, the agency or production house will hire a food stylist who knows how to attractively prepare and present food for the camera.

Sketches and Plans

If sets are to be built, the video or film director prepares plans using the same process as for a dramatic production: sketches, construction drawings, and bids. Very short time frames may preclude the construction drawing process, and the shop may have to put together stock flats from a sketch on a paper towel, not the best way to go.

Money Matters

Some set art directors who specialize in commercials contract their services for a flat fee, which may include construction costs, helpers, and props. This is OK for an experienced person to tackle, but if you are just starting out, it's better to have the production house handle these elements. Never spend your own money because it's frequently difficult to get it back again.

HERE'S THE SCRIPT

Now that the ground rules are entrenched in your mind, read the script.

HUFFNAGEL, TWITCHELL, AND BURNS ADVERTISING

30-SECOND TELEVISION SPOT #345
CLIENT: ACME DETERGENTS
PRODUCT: JIFFY CLEANER
CREATIVE DIRECTOR: DAWN DAILY
ART DIRECTOR: PAT TERRIFIC

SETTING: HIGH-RISE CONDO KITCHEN IN MIDTOWN,
U.S.A.
TIME: WINTER WEEKDAY, 6:30 PM
CU HOUSEHUSBAND BRUCE'S SWEATY HARASSED FACE.
CAMERA PULLS BACK, REVEALING BRUCE SCRUBBING
THE SINK BASEBOARD WITH STEEL WOOL.
FLEUR, BRUCE'S WIFE, ENTERS CARRYING A POWER
BRIEFCASE, WHICH SHE SLAMS DOWN ON THE BREAK-
FAST BAR.

                    FLEUR
What are you doing, Bruce?

BRUCE STANDS UP INTO 2-SHOT

                    BRUCE
Just trying to get this scuff mark off the
baseboard, that's all. It's been some day!
First, the couch didn't come from Bloomie's.
Then, Roger called and talked for an hour and
a half about our fishing trip, and then...

                    FLEUR
Never mind. I've got just the thing!

CUT TO: CU FLEUR TAKING SPRAY BOTTLE OF JIFFY
CLEANER OUT OF HER BRIEFCASE, HOLDING THE
LABEL SIDE TO CAMERA.

Jiffy will make that mark disappear like
magic!...and won't leave a stain!

                    BRUCE
You think of everything, honey! Why don't you
slip into something more comfortable and whip
up some pasta?

BRUCE'S HAND CARESSES FLEUR'S HAND HOLDING THE
JIFFY BOTTLE. MUSIC: ROMANTIC VIOLINS

                    FLEUR
Never mind the pasta, darling. Just take care
of that baseboard.

DISSOLVE TO MOON RISING BEHIND SKYSCRAPERS.
MUSIC RISES AS CAMERA ZOOMS INTO MOON WITH
IMAGE OF JIFFY BOTTLE.

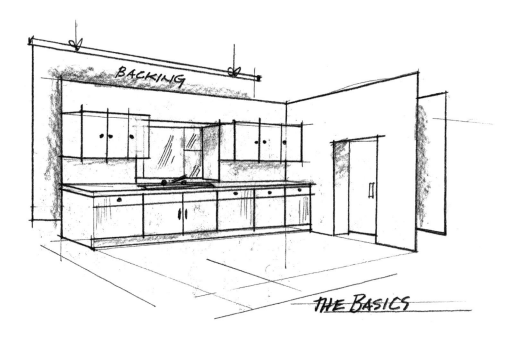

THE BASIC SET

Commercials present a lot of information in a short period of time. Each set element contributes to viewers' perceptions of the characters, environment, and above all, the product's virtues. In some cases, the product is the atmosphere created by a setting that communicates elegance, speed, efficiency, or other positive attributes.

Remember that you need to give the *impression* of a high-rise condominium building, but do not need to build the entire building; just a kitchen in the building. Select some set elements that communicate *height* and *apartment building* such as a window view showing that the building is high, and a doorway through which Fleur enters which shows a hallway not found in a tract home. Start with two walls set at a right angle to each other. One wall needs a door and the other wall needs a window, sink, and cabinets.

Set Improvements

Looks pretty dull, doesn't it? Let's improve this set. Add visual interest by putting the sink in a freestanding island with a work surface. This will bring Bruce's problem scuff toward easy camera access and add three-dimensional interest to the set. Because the sink does not need running water, the island unit's plumbing

IMPROVED KITCHEN

does not have to work and the unit can be positioned to satisfy the director's every whim. The previous sink-below-the-window approach would have worked, but it would not have given the impression that Bruce and Fleur are up-scale people or make the director smile.

Turning our attention to the former sink wall, it holds the window through which we see the skyscrapers and moon, and the custom-built counter and trendy-color refrigerator, stovetop, expensive cannisters, and kitchen appliances which a couple like Bruce and Fleur would have but are actually rented from a property rental house by the set decorator. Remember that a couple like Bruce and Fleur would hardly have a set of cannisters shaped like teddy bears.

What about the Hallway?

Find out what elements exist in high-rise condo hallways. Perhaps the service elevator doors are across from the kitchen door, or a stairway with an EXIT sign. If the city-at-night backing you rent shows the skyscrapers from ground level, roll it up from the bottom to just show the across-the-street building's upper floors.

Remember the Scuff

Pay close attention to the crucial scuff area. See that the carpenters pay meticulous attention to this area because it will be seen in extreme closeup, which can reveal sloppy corner joints or flaws in the cabinet materials. The agency people will scrutinize the area where their product will work its magic. They will probably hire a kitchen stain and mess expert to create a scuff mark that can be easily removed.

DESIGNING OTHER ENVIRONMENTS

In the preceding photograph, you see a commercial set for another cleaning product that gives a different impression than our high-rise example. Notice the lighting. A cheery shaft of sunlight pours through the window and light haze from a haze generator provides atmosphere between the window and the backing. The window design, ceiling beams, and set decoration objects give the sense of a different type of owner than the other example couple. Notice the economical construction, which includes only the elements to be seen on camera, and the production clutter of the lighting instruments and crew.

On the first shoot day, the art director hears a lot of comments — both positive and negative. Be flexible, willing to listen, and willing to change some things. As we have said before, personal taste enters into projects. If you have done the best job you can, be satisfied with that, and learn from whatever mistakes you may have made.

●

In the preceding chapters, we have seen examples of design and production successes as well as problems. The only way to get some real-life experience is to begin working in the art direction profession. Turn to the next chapter for some helpful tips on how to prepare and where to look.

21

HOW TO GET STARTED
AND WHERE TO LOOK

Where to begin? Let's look at some allied fields and areas that may not set you to work designing sets right away, but are on the fringes of show work.

Set decorator Deborah Lakeman started as a page (messenger) at NBC; she says:

> I studied interior design at the same time. Interior design is different from set decoration because it takes place over a longer period of time. The design part of it is similar, but a set decorator needs to know what the camera sees. Then I got a job as a production assistant and learned from the bottom up. That led to working for art directors as a shopper and then at CBS as an assistant to a set decorator. I got to know the prophouses, which are our main resource.

Colin Irwin started his career as an actor when he was nine years old:

> When I got into high school, I migrated into set design and lighting. After high school, I went to USC for a while and then started designing for waiver theater (99-seat houses not covered by union rules) where you have no time and no money! I was lucky to get $200 for designing a play with a $300 budget. I did a music video and eventually landed a job with an art director I continued to work for. It's been a slow progression of meeting people, learning skills, and being there learning.

GET YOUR FOOT IN THE DOOR

If you attend a college or university with a television and/or film department, present yourself at their doorstep. If you are an art student, see if the film and video department welcomes help with sets, lighting, and other production tasks. Learn as much as you can about the job they ask you to do, as well as lighting, sound, camera, writing, and carpentry. Your skills can complement the areas you want to learn about.

Windows and Interiors

Department store display departments are excellent places to use your three-dimensional design ability. The interesting presentation of store merchandise compares to the way sets present actors in a drama.

Come on Now, Smile!

Commercial photography offers other opportunities. Many still photographers employ *stylists* who collect props and arrange settings. In some cases, the stylist scouts locations for the photographer and makes alterations and additions.

You're Getting Closer

Small theater groups welcome talented people to help with scenic work, especially if they show up when it's time to do the work. Because budgets are small, little theater set design requires much improvisation, a useful skill to develop no matter what the budget size.

Are You Connected?

Cable television systems serve most communities and offer the use of their facilities to citizens who wish to put on their own programs. Many cable operators offer free instruction to anyone willing to spend a few class hours learning how to operate the equipment.

GETTING YOUR ACT TOGETHER

When you go to the big city to seek your fortune, you will discover many other people who are trying to do the same thing. The better prepared you are, the better your chances. Here are some suggestions.

Your Portfolio Samples

Look at your sketches and photos and select the ones that best represent your work. Slides are awkward to present for viewing, so get prints made and mount them, as well as other flat work, on the same size mat boards. The neatness shown by your presentation says a lot about your work habits to a prospective employer. Fold blueprints to manageable size. Rolled prints are troublesome to show, because they curl when unrolled. Carry your samples in a weatherproof, zipper-closed case. To show your model-making skills, use photographs.

The Résumé

Prepare a simple one-page résumé listing your education, work history, and other relevant skills. Include your address and phone number, of course. Remember, prospective employers see many résumés, are busy, and don't have time to work their way through a tricky presentation such as a clever gift box. Have cards printed to accompany your résumé, and you do have an answering machine, don't you?

WHERE TO LOOK

Now that you see how to prepare a portfolio and résumé, let's look at where you can put all this equipment to use.

Opportunities in Video Design

The line between film and video production companies has blurred, because television uses both mediums. First, we will see where to begin looking for jobs in video.

Local Television

A small station in a local market is a good place to start. Because an art director in this situation does a little bit of everything, a designer with a modest amount of experience can focus interests and learn what set and graphic design require on a daily basis. Local public broadcasting stations maintain staffs of production people, and welcome volunteer workers as well.

Most local stations have a network affiliation; that is, they are not owned by a network but agree to run a certain amount of programming produced by a network. Other stations are independent: They also produce some of their own programs, but buy syndicated material from independent producers. Art directors generally have more design freedom at independent or affiliated stations. A network-owned station art director generally has to follow a network-created graphic design program.

Network Television

The commercial television networks headquarters are in New York and Los Angeles. They produce programming, as well as buy from independent producers. In the past, when networks produced many of their own programs, they maintained larger staffs of art directors and graphic designers than they do now. Union rules cover jobs at these facilities.

Independent Producers

Art directors commonly work on a freelance basis for the companies that sell programming to networks and independent stations. Some of the larger independents employ staff art directors.

Corporate Video

Some large corporations maintain film and video production departments that produce information programs for use within the company. These programs present training, technical, corporate news, and employee-relations material.

Motion Picture Opportunities

Some designers move from video to motion picture work, where the pay is better and the productions more challenging. Many motion picture studios still employ staffs of art directors who may not work on a permanent basis, but are hired for limited periods. Feature films produced with studio facilities, but not studio productions, hire their own production designers and art directors who work on a contract basis.

The Union

As in many other work areas, technicians and artists banded together to form organizations to oversee working conditions and salaries. Producers who sign union contracts are required to hire union members as long as they are available. Some producers work out alternative agreements that allow them to hire outside the union for certain jobs. Inquire locally for information on requirements for union membership.

Nonunion Productions

Many production designers and art directors start out working on nonunion productions, and many continue on this path. Without set rules, designers can work out their own agreements with producers. Some agents handle freelance art directors who have proven credits and good future career possibilities.

Opportunities in Other Areas

Now that equipment is easily transportable and location filming is popular, most states and cities have film offices that are responsible for attracting and helping film companies. These offices also maintain lists of available personnel and services, including art directors.

HOW TO LOOK

Production designer Larry Miller looks for staff members who have certain qualities:

> I like to find people who can get along with each other, and are good at follow up because the work is hard and the hours are disgusting. When I hire art directors, I must have people who are computer savvy, because we use the system to watch the budget.

Line Up Interviews

Ask for names of prospective employers and knowledgeable friends from people you already know. Look in phone book yellow pages and use specialized film and video directories. Get names of department heads and call them for appointments. Mass résumé mailings sometimes get results, especially if mailed to specific people.

Research the Company Needs

A video or film supervising art director does not want to see examples of jewelry design or photographs of sunlight slanting through a picket fence, no matter how versatile you think you are. Find out what the company does and present yourself accordingly. Show examples specific to the prospective employer, a reason for creating a looseleaf portfolio. Edit your samples based on the demands of the interview.

When the Phone Rings

Be on time for interviews and better still, a few minutes early! Dress conservatively; you have not met the person you are going to see and don't know what to expect. Green hair, a tee-shirt, and jeans might not fit the company's image.

Because you have done some research, show that you know something about your prospective employer and the company. Present your résumé and wait till it's scanned. Answer questions honestly. Your interviewer might call the references at the bottom of the page.

Don't give a guided tour through your samples, but fill in information if asked. Express thanks and leave your card along with your résumé; many prospective employers say they will keep it on file, and most of them do. If the response, "Your work is very nice but we haven't any openings right now" discourages you, don't let it bother you too much. Just line up another interview when you get home. Your phone may ring tomorrow when a new production comes along.

●

Now that your head is reeling with all this advice, turn to the last section for some words of encouragement.

FROM THE AUTHOR

I have tried to present a realistic view of the production design and art direction professions by drawing on my own experience and by quoting other designers who have practical experience. This book is not intended to be a detailed textbook about design, but an overview of the work and the opportunities, and how to begin taking advantage of them.

I have enjoyed and been excited by the magic since I saw my first stage show with a couple of comedians rowing a boat across what appeared to my six-year-old eyes as real water. "How did they do that?" I wondered. I have spent a major part of my life finding out how stage and film works and being a part of creations that enhance our lives and stimulate our imaginations.

My hope is that you will get whatever you are seeking from this book and that you will find as much enjoyment and satisfaction as I have from working in the film and video world.

●

INDEX

•